THE GREAT COOKS' GUIDE TO

Pasta & Noodle Dishes

GREAT COOKS' LIBRARY

Appetizers
Breads
Cakes
Chickens, Ducks & Other Poultry
Children's Cookery
Clay Cookery
Cookies
Crêpes & Soufflés
Fish Cookery
Flambéing Desserts
Ice Cream & Other Frozen Desserts
Omelets from Around the World
Pasta & Noodle Dishes
Pies & Tarts
Rice Cookery
Salads
Soups
Vegetable Cookery
Wine Drinks
Woks, Steamers & Fire Pots

America's leading food authorities share their home-tested recipes and expertise on cooking equipment and techniques

THE GREAT COOKS' GUIDE TO

Pasta
& Noodle Dishes

RANDOM HOUSE, NEW YORK

Front Cover (left to right, top to bottom): Linguine or Fettuccine with Fresh Tomato-Pesto Sauce, page 25.

Back Cover (left to right, top to bottom): *(glass containers courtesy Bloomingdale's);* Lasagne with Fennel Sausages, page 28 *(lasagne pan courtesy Copco, Inc.);* Stir-Fried Noodles with Shrimp and Vegetables, page 53 *(cheese grater courtesy Hoffritz).*

Interior Photographs: Page 3 (top), *manual pasta machine courtesy Berarducci Brothers;* Page 3 (bottom), *electric pasta machine courtesy Gary Valenti;* Page 4 (top), *pasta knife and double-wheeled cutter courtesy Rowoco, Inc.;* Page 7 (bottom), *plastic cheese grater courtesy Scan Plast Industries, stainless-steel cheese grater courtesy Hoffritz.*

Book Design by Milton Glaser, Inc.

Cover Photograph by Richard Jeffery

Food Styling by Lucy Wing
Props selected by Yvonne McHarg and Beard Glaser Wolf Ltd.

 Published in the United States by Random House, Inc., New York and simultaneously in Canada by Random House of Canada Limited, Toronto.

Library of Congress Cataloguing in Publication Data

The Great Cooks' Guide to Pasta and Noodle Dishes.
(The Great Cooks' Library)
1. Cookery (Macaroni) I. Series.
TX809.M17G7 641.8'22 77-90239
ISBN: 0-394-73602-8

Manufactured in the United States of America
2 4 6 8 9 7 5 3
First Edition

We have gathered together some of the great cooks in this country to share their recipes—and their expertise—with you. As you read the recipes, you will find that in certain cases techniques will vary. This is as it should be: Cooking is a highly individual art, and our experts have arrived at their own personal methods through years of experience in the kitchen.

THE EDITORS

SENIOR EDITORS

Wendy Afton Rieder
Kate Slate

ASSOCIATE EDITORS

Lois Bloom
Susan Lipke

EDITORIAL ASSISTANT

Christopher Carter

PRODUCTION MANAGER

Emily Aronson

EDITORIAL STAFF

Mardee Haidin
Michael Sears
Patricia Thomas

CONTRIBUTORS

Introduction by Lyn Stallworth

Eliza and Joshua Baer have worked in various phases of the restaurant business on the West Coast and are currently planning a cookbook.

Michael Batterberry, author of several books on food, art and social history, is also a painter, and is editor and food critic for a number of national magazines. He has taught at James Beard's cooking classes in New York and many of his original recipes have appeared in *House & Garden, House Beautiful* and *Harper's Bazaar.*

Paula J. Buchholz is the regional co-ordinator for the National Culinary Apprenticeship Program. She has been a food writer for the *Detroit Free Press* and for the *San Francisco Examiner.*

Giuliano Bugialli, author of *The Fine Art of Italian Cooking,* is co-founder and teacher of Cooking in Florence, a program conducted in Italy. He also has a cooking school in New York.

Elizabeth Schneider Colchie is a noted food consultant who has done extensive recipe development and testing as well as research into the history of foods and cookery. She was on the editorial staff of *The Cooks' Catalogue* and *The International Cooks' Catalogue* and has written numerous articles for such magazines as *Gourmet, House & Garden* and *Family Circle.*

Carol Cutler, who has been a food columnist for the *Washington Post*, is a graduate of the Cordon Bleu and L'Ecole des Trois Gourmands in Paris. She is the author of *Haute Cuisine for Your Heart's Delight*, and *The Six-Minute Soufflé and Other Culinary Delights.* She has also written for *House & Garden, American Home* and *Harper's Bazaar.*

Florence Fabricant is a free-lance writer, reporting on restaurants and food for *The New York Times, New York* magazine and other publications. She was on the staff of *The Cooks' Catalogue* and editor of the paperback edition. She also contributed to *The International Cooks' Catalogue* and *Where to Eat in America.*

Emanuel and Madeline Greenberg co-authored *Whiskey in the Kitchen* and are consultants to the food and beverage industry. Emanuel, a home economist, is a regular contributor to the food columns of *Playboy* magazine. Both contribute to *House Beautiful, Harper's Bazaar* and *Travel & Leisure.*

Mireille Johnston, the author of *The Cuisine of the Sun,* a cookbook of Provençal specialties, is currently completing a book on the cooking of Burgundy, *The Cuisine of the Rose.*

Alma Lach holds a Diplôme de Cordon Bleu from Paris and has served as food editor for the *Chicago Sun-Times.* She is author of *How's and Why's of French Cooking* and *Cooking à la Cordon Bleu* as well as many other cookbooks and articles on food. She directs the Alma Lach Cooking School in Chicago and is currently the television chef on the P.B.S. program "Over Easy."

Jeanne Lesem, Family Editor of United Press International, is the author of *The Pleasures of Preserving and Pickling.*

Florence S. Lin has been teaching Chinese cooking at the China Institute in New York for 17 years. She is the author of *Florence Lin's Chinese Regional Cookbook* and *Florence Lin's Chinese Vegetarian Cookbook* and was the chief food consultant for the *Cooking of China* in Time-Life Books' *Foods of the World* series.

Nan Mabon, a freelance food writer and cooking teacher in New York City, is also the cook for a private executive dining room on Wall Street. She studied at the Cordon Bleu in London.

Mitsuo Masuzawa has been a chef at the Kitcho Restaurant in New York City since 1970.

Gloria Bley Miller is the author of *Learn Chinese Cooking in Your Own Kitchen* and *The Thousand Recipe Chinese Cookbook.*

Maurice Moore-Betty, owner-operator of The Civilized Art Cooking School, food consultant and restaurateur, is author of *Cooking for Occasions, The Maurice Moore-Betty Cooking School Book of Fine Cooking* and *The Civilized Art of Salad Making.*

Jane Moulton, a food writer for the *Plain Dealer* in Cleveland, took her degree in foods and nutrition. As well as reporting on culinary matters and reviewing food-related books for the *Plain Dealer*, she has worked in recipe development, public relations and catering.

Paul Rubinstein is the author of *Feasts for Two, The Night Before Cookbook* and *Feasts for Twelve (or More).* He is a stockbroker and the son of pianist Artur Rubinstein.

Maria Luisa Scott and Jack Denton Scott co-authored the popular *Complete Book of Pasta* and have also written many other books on food, including *Informal Dinners for Easy Entertaining, Mastering Microwave Cooking, The Best of the Pacific Cookbook,* and *Cook Like a Peasant, Eat Like a King.* With the renowned chef Antoine Gilly, they wrote *Feast of France.*

Kate Slate is a Senior Editor of The Great Cooks' Library series, as well as *The International Cooks' Catalogue* and *Where to Eat in America.*

Raymond Sokolov, author of *The Saucier's Apprentice,* is a freelance writer with a particular interest in food.

Ruth Spear is the author of *The East Hampton Cookbook* and writes occasional pieces on food for *New York* magazine. She is currently at work on a new cookbook.

Paula Wolfert, author of *Mediterranean Cooking* and *Couscous and Other Good Food from Morocco,* is also a cooking teacher and consultant. She has written articles for *Vogue* and other magazines.

Nicola Zanghi is the owner-chef of Restaurant Zanghi in Glen Cove, New York. He started his apprenticeship under his father at the age of thirteen, and is a graduate of two culinary colleges. He has been an instructor at the Cordon Bleu school in New York City.

Contents

NOODLE DISHES

Pasta

Pasta and noodles may seem humble fare, but to many they occupy a position of greater importance and respect than such gourmet prizes as truffles and caviar: Tibetans offer noodles to the gods; Chinese eat them at the New Year because their length is symbolic of longevity; and the Italians have honored pasta with its very own museum, the *Museo Storico degli Spaghetti.*

To almost every culture on the globe, some form of noodle is soul food: inexpensive, quickly made, nutritious and wholly satisfying. In Thailand, vendors hawk crisp fried rice noodles to theater crowds and shoppers at outdoor markets; Japanese fill up the breaks between meals with steaming bowls of hot noodles in winter, and refreshing dishes of chilled noodles in summer. In America, *kugels*, the sweet noodle puddings that originated in the Jewish enclaves of Eastern Europe, grace Friday night tables from Oregon to Ohio. *Mein* (noodles to you) are the primary staple of Northern China; *chao mein* (chow mein in English) means fried noodles. And macaroni and cheese is almost as American as the hot dog. This basic food appears in endless variety around the world, but it took Italy to raise pasta making to a national art.

Pasta Trivia. Pasta is any product made from pure water and semolina, and literally means paste, or dough. Semolina is fine flour milled from the heart of duram wheat, the hardest wheat grown. Eggs and sometimes oil can be added to the basic dough, both for factory-made and homemade pasta. (When eggs are included, the pasta product may be referred to as noodles.) Although Italians count over 600 pasta shapes, one expert has succinctly defined pasta as fitting into four basic forms: ribbons, tubes, cords and "special shapes." The dough is essentially the same, but the thickness, thinness, curves and grooves of each shape will determine how a pasta will hold sauce, crunch between the teeth, and manage to have a character all its own.

Sizes range from the almost microscopic *perline* ("little pearls") for soup, to the broad rippled bands called *lasagne riccie* (*riccie* means "curly") that add substance and definition to a family Sunday dinner. To name just a few of the shapes in between these two, there are *farfalle* ("butterflies") usually called "bowties" in this country; *ditalini* ("little thimbles"), which are small tubes of macaroni cut in short lengths; and the dramatically named *elettrici rigati* ("grooved electric wire"). Macaroni and spaghetti, by the way, are the names of pasta shapes, not generic groupings.

The origins of pasta in Italy are somewhat clouded. For generations we've been told that Marco Polo brought pasta to Italy on his return from China in about the year 1270. It's a nice story, but not a true one. The Spaghetti Museum has proof that regulations for the size and shape of various pastas were in existence as early as 1200, years before Marco's celebrated journey...or even his birth! The Chinese of his day certainly were eating noodles, but the two traditions grew separately. Among the marvels of the strange land he visited, Marco probably found that a nice dish of noodles was a comforting reminder of home!

Modernday Italians eat pasta twice a day, every day of the year (62 pounds per capita annually), and insist that it's not fattening. And taken in the Italian way, it isn't; one- to two-ounce servings of sauced pasta at the midday meal are followed by vegetables or a salad, plus cheese and fruit. There is no meat course. In the evening, a broth, with a little *pastina* to enliven it, precedes the meat course.

Moderation, of course, is the key to having one's pasta and a fine figure as well. Ah, moderation! So easy to talk of, so difficult to practice, when the dish is spaghetti with clam sauce, or *fettuccine* dripping with butter and cheese. It's so difficult to refuse a second helping, or even a third ...but, say the Italians, pasta should whet the appetite, not destroy it. You should consume every morsel on your plate with delight, long for more, and *not* get it. That's because, traditionally, other food will follow.

Storebought or Homemade? *Pasta secca*, the air-dried commercial product made in hundreds of shapes (usually without eggs) is an excellent food—economical and quickly prepared. The best pastas are imported from Italy and are a deep ivory color that comes from the hardest of semolinas. However, to the true lover of pasta, *pasta fresca*, usually enriched with eggs and cut into ribbon-like shapes or stuffed, is incomparable. (Ribbons, incidentally, are more common in the North of Italy; southerners prefer tubular pasta.)

Some zealots insist that *pasta fresca* be made by hand, kneaded until the dough forms a smooth elastic ball, and then rolled out with a long rolling pin and cut with a pasta knife. Only that way, they state, will the sauce cling properly to the strands. If you, the cook, find joy in the operation, by all means go ahead and make fresh pasta in the time-honored Northern Italian way. However, many people, just as demanding, prefer to use a pasta machine, blessing its speed and finding no real difference in the end result. Manually operated machines knead the dough between smooth rollers; then, when it is ready for its final shape, another set of rollers cuts it into the desired size, such as *fettuccine*. One pasta machine even has an attachment to turn out the delicate filaments called angel's hair, as well as a wavy-edged cutter for *lasagne riccie*.

The electric pasta machine works in the same way as the manual ones, except that electricity rather than hand-cranking passes the dough through the mangle-like rollers. At first thought, an electric pasta machine may seem a sinful extravagance, but the following end most certainly justifies the indulgence: With the aid of a food processor, a batch of pasta can be prepared in 15 minutes. In addition, an electric machine fitted with

Pasta machine. Arduous kneading and rolling of stiff pasta dough can be circumvented with a device like this one. Adjustable metal rollers knead the dough and then press it thinner and thinner as it is fed through the machine 8 to 12 times. It then cuts the pasta into fine or broad strips.

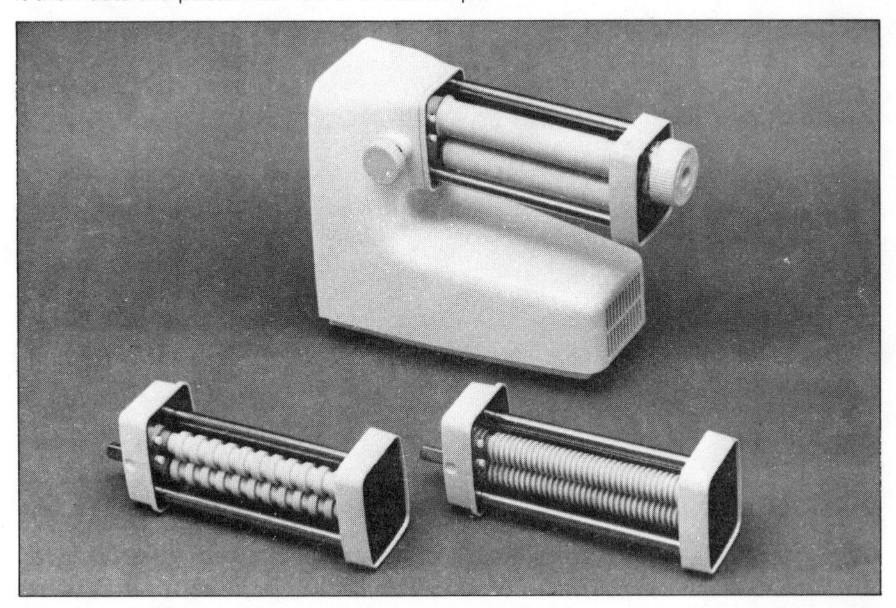

Electric pasta machine. The nylon rollers on this machine produce less slick, more absorbent pasta than steel rollers do, and since they are exposed, they are easy to clean. Suction cups hold the machine steady; two cutting rollers turn out thin or broad strips of pasta or noodles.

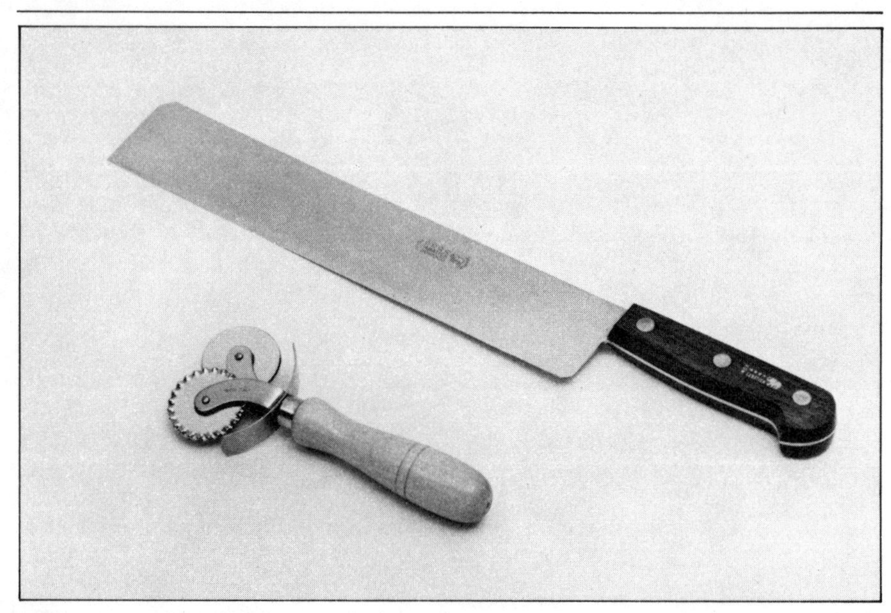

Pasta knife and double wheel. A large, flat knife with a straight, sharp edge is useful for cutting fresh pasta dough. To cut *fettuccine*, the dough is rolled up loosely and sliced at ¼" intervals. A double pasta wheel will cut jagged or straight edges on noodles, lasagne or ravioli without tearing or distorting the dough.

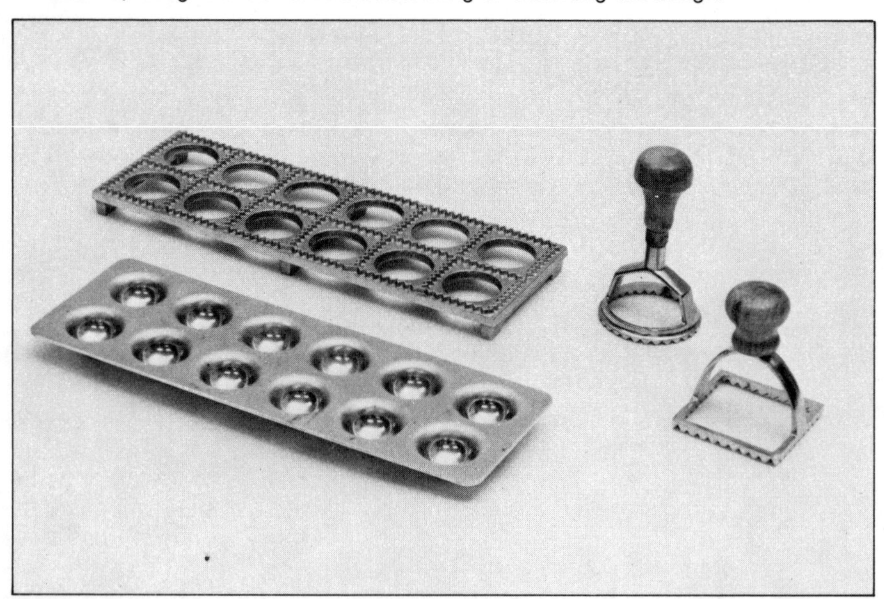

Ravioli trays and stuffed-pasta stamps. Metal trays make several ravioli at once. One tray presses pockets into the dough, the other cuts neat, pinked squares out of it once the second sheet of dough has been laid on top. Round and square individual cutters cut and seal two layers of dough into *agnolotti* and ravioli.

nylon rollers will produce a pasta with a surface that will "grab" and hold the sauce.

Once the pasta has been kneaded and rolled into a flat, thin sheet—either with a rolling pin or machine—it can be cut with a pasta knife (for long, straight strands), or pastry wheel or jagger, into various shapes. In fact, pasta shapes that are to be stuffed (such as ravioli or *cappelletti*) should be cut and filled while the dough is still flexible. If the pasta is to be cut by machine, however, the dough should be allowed to relax for about 15 minutes before being run through the cutting rollers. In either case, the final pasta forms should ideally be allowed to dry, on a lightly floured cloth, for an hour before cooking.

In addition to the machines that do the majority of the work, other aids will help you achieve authentic pasta shapes. With a dough cutter (available with a smooth or jagged wheel, or both), you can cut strips to any width desired, or make pasta shapes with pinked edges. Ravioli cutters of various types will turn out those little stuffed pockets with speed and professional precision. Some tray-type *raviolatori* (ravioli makers) will produce a dozen or so ravioli at once; others resemble cookie cutters and will make individual square ravioli or round *agnolotti*. There is even one marvelous contraption into which dough and stuffing are fed on a conveyor belt, to emerge on the other side as individual ravioli. Or finally, you may amuse yourself with a modern version of a wonderful, traditional Italian kitchen aid called a *chitarra* (called a "guitar" in Italian because of its resemblance to the musical instrument). A sheet of dough pressed through the instrument's wire strings will emerge as spaghetti strands.

Cooking Pasta. Now that you've made *pasta fresca*—or opted for one of the myriad dried varieties—you'll need to cook it. For this you should have a large, sturdy, deep pot so that the pasta can swim unfettered, each piece whirling and turning in its water-bath. Fresh pasta will cook more rapidly than dried, and fresh pasta made at home with all-purpose flour instead of semolina will cook faster still. Of course, the larger and thicker the shape, the *longer* it will take. But fresh or dried, thick or thin, pasta needs lots and lots of water to cook properly: at least seven quarts for each pound of pasta.

Bring the water to a rolling boil, and only then add the amount of salt called for (one food authority states that if salt and water boil together for any length of time, the pasta will smell of carbolic acid!). At the same time, you may also want to add a tablespoon of olive oil, which will insure that the strands do not stick together. Then gently drop in the pasta, all at one time, stirring with a fork (a wooden fork is preferred as metal tends to break or pierce the strands or shapes). Push down until all of the pasta is submerged, then give it a few delicate swirls to be sure that the pasta is separated. Now, watch the pot!

Timing is all-important. In principle, three to five minutes will suffice for homemade pasta, and five to eight minutes for storebought. However, the only way to be sure that your pasta emerges *al dente*—"to the tooth"—is to use your *tooth* to test it. It should have a little bit of spring, with the center cooked through; but it should never, never be mushy. Keep an eye on the pot, and start fishing out bits to test when the pasta is nearing the end of its cooking time. Don't rely on the cooking times printed on the boxes; they are invariably too long. (Most manufacturers of imported pasta play it safe and don't even suggest how long the time should be.) Pasta that will also be baked, however, should be slightly undercooked.

As soon as the pasta is done, remove it from the water. For large pieces, such as *rigatoni* or *ziti*, drain the pot into a heavy, stable colander. As an alternative to pouring steaming hot water and pasta into a colander, you might want to use a spaghetti pot, which comes with its own perforated colander insert. The pasta is cooked in, and then lifted out with, the insert. Many pasta *aficionados* insist that the pasta will get cold in the time it takes to drain. One solution for strand-type pasta is to use a pasta rake. The wooden teeth on the rake snag the pasta and transport it directly from the pot to a *warmed* serving bowl or plate. For successful pasta, the importance of warming all dishes cannot be overemphasized. Compact shapes can be moved from pot to serving bowl with a large perforated scoop or ladle. Pasta that is to be sauced immediately, should really not be rinsed with cold water. Although the cold bath *will* stop the cooking process, it will also make the pasta sticky.

Sauces. Although Americans are becoming more aware of the variety in pasta dishes, far too many of us still think of pasta as positively naked without a coating of tomato sauce. Nothing could be farther from the truth. Some of the finest sauces are also the simplest, unkissed by even a hint of tomato. A simple, quick and easy dressing made of herbed oil and garlic suits spaghetti to perfection; and *fettuccine* with fresh seafood is incomparable. *Fettuccine*, brought steaming to the table and tossed at the last minute with butter, cheese and black pepper is a classic treatment of this pasta. (The dish is now named for Alfredo, a 20th century restaurateur who was lucky enough to impress Douglas Fairbanks and Mary Pickford with his rendition of *fettuccine al parmigiano e burro*. In its present incarnation, *fettuccine all'Alfredo* includes heavy cream.)

Not that the tomato does not hold an honored place as a pasta partner; it certainly does, and some of the best tomato sauces are very quickly made. Several are even raw! Try *spaghettini* with chopped fresh tomato, garlic, basil, oil and lemon juice. Dusted with a little grated cheese, this dish is a boon to diners and easy on the summer cook. Ripe, homegrown tomatoes are the best. But if all you can get are so-called "hard ripe" tomatoes sold in little plastic coffins in the supermarket, canned Italian plum tomatoes should be used instead.

Grated Cheese. Not every pasta dish calls for grated cheese—in fact, Italians never eat it with seafood or marinara sauce. When you *do* use cheese for Italian pasta dishes, it should be good, hard, well-aged Italian grating cheese. Aged Parmesan is the choicest; it should be at least two years old for its flavor to have ripened fully. Unfortunately, the price is becoming prohibitive. *Asiago*, a nutty yet mild cheese somewhat difficult to find, is also excellent. Romano is salty and sharp; if you buy it, you will

Pasta pot and colander, rake and tongs. To boil pasta, a large pot is essential. If it comes with a perforated liner as this one does, it is even better for safely removing hot pasta. Or, for spaghetti and other long noodles, a long-handled wooden spaghetti rake is also handy. The tongs are for tossing and serving spaghetti.

Cheese graters. Here are three ways of dealing with hard Italian grating cheeses: A metal mill with a crank to turn the grating cylinder, the handle conveniently holding the cheese in place; a colorful plastic mill to put right on the table; and a stainless-steel grater with a bowl handily attached to catch the cheese.

Stainless-steel tomato press. Squeeze tomatoes speedily to a pulp with this handy *spremipomodoro* that clamps firmly to the counter, strains out seeds and skin and sends fresh puree down the chute as fast as you can load the hopper and pull the crank handle.

Noodle board and pin. To make noodles by hand, use a large, hardwood board and a very long and thin, heavy rolling pin. Season a new pin by rubbing a little olive oil into it and wiping it dry. Then dust the board and pin with flour, and lift and turn the dough as you roll it out, adding flour when it shows signs of sticking.

probably want to mix it half-and-half with Parmesan. Grated cheese is at its best when it is freshly grated, as exposure to air causes it to quickly lose its character. Some cooks feel that the flavor goes so fast that the cheese should only be grated at the table, and therefore equip each diner with an individual grater. The grated cheese sold prepackaged in supermarkets is no more than costly sawdust.

Other Noodles. You won't have real Italian pasta without semolina, but other noodles are made from a staggering variety of starches. Human ingenuity, combined with a need for economy, has produced noodles from rice, seaweed, soy and mung beans, chick-peas, buckwheat and numerous tuberous roots, from manioc to potatoes. Nearly every culture has found a way to mix some kind of flour with water and make noodles, or their very close relatives, dumplings.

The noodle closest to most American hearts and stomachs is the so-called egg noodle—a term that does not distinguish it from *pasta all'uovo*, which is made with eggs, but which conjures up images of rich, Pennsylvania Dutch noodle dishes. This noodle heritage comes to us from Germany, Austria, Poland, Hungary and Russia, where noodles (made with eggs) are served boiled, baked, sautéed, or in puddings, and very often sweet. In the average Hungarian household, for example, a sweet noodle dish may be served several times a week, as a main course or a dessert. In Germany, noodles are tossed with butter or the omnipresent bacon fat and dusted with nutmeg, poppyseeds, ground walnuts or paprika, or made more substantial with bacon or ham.

Other countries have their noodles as well—French *nouilles*, Greek *orzo* and *pastichio*, North African *couscous*—but the real rivals of Italy as the world's pasta center are China and Japan. Noodles are the staple of Northern China, where wheat rather than rice is grown, and have been a part of the Chinese diet (some say) for more than 6000 years. Chinese noodles are made with rice or wheat flours, come in various thicknesses, are sold dried and fresh, and are served in soup, deep-fried, or boiled and then stir-fried. Noodle dough is also used to wrap various fillings to make wontons, egg rolls and *chaotzu* (fried dumplings). In Japan, noodles are second only to rice in the diet, and are sold in restaurants, soup bars and by street vendors. Fresh and dried Japanese noodles are made of wheat (fat *udon* and skinny *somen*) and buckwheat (*soba*). Both China and Japan have another kind of noodle (quite unlike Western-style pastas) called—variously—bean thread, cellophane noodles or shining noodles. These "translucent" noodles are made of soy or mung bean flour, or the flour of a taro-like tuber called devil's tongue. When steeped in boiling water, the noodles become transparent, chewy and very slippery.

Many Chinese and Japanese noodles are now being sold on a mass-market level, having previously been confined to small China- and Japantown grocery stores. In the United States, however, the government has insisted that a noodle cannot be *called* a noodle unless it contains egg; therefore, many of the eggless varieties of Oriental noodles are sold under the unfortunate handle of "alimentary paste." The offputting name notwithstanding, they are authentic and delicious.

Italian Pasta Dishes

PASTA DOUGH

Maria Luisa Scott and Jack Denton Scott

About 1 pound

It has become relatively simple these days to make homemade pasta since the number and variety of pasta machines on the market has grown considerably. When we were writing our first guide to pasta, *The Complete Book of Pasta*, most of our pasta recipes called for muscle. The new pasta machines come with metal or nylon rollers that will quickly turn out a variety of thicknesses of ''sheet,'' the technical term for pasta dough that has been rolled. Most machines have six settings, adjustable by a knob, and additional cutting rollers that cut the pasta sheet into various widths. The recipe that follows is an old family ''receipt,'' which, for us, at least, produces palatable pasta.

2 CUPS ALL-PURPOSE FLOUR
2 EGGS
1 EGG WHITE
1 TABLESPOON OLIVE OIL
1 TEASPOON SALT
2 TABLESPOONS WARM WATER

1. Sift the flour onto a pastry board, make a well in its center, break the eggs into the well, then add the egg white, olive oil, salt and half of the water. Using your hands, blend well, gathering together and kneading until the dough can be formed into a ball.

   Note: If the flour doesn't seem to mix well or hold together as it is kneaded, add a little more warm water, slowly. Or, if the dough is too soft, add a small amount of flour.

2. Turn the pastry board over (or scrape the working surface clean), flour it lightly and knead the dough well. It should take about 15 minutes to obtain a smooth, elastic dough. Form into a ball, cover with a bowl and let it rest for 30 minutes.
3. Divide the dough into three balls. One at a time, place each ball on a clean, lightly floured pastry board and roll it out into as thin a sheet as possible. This takes some doing. Use a long, heavy rolling pin—and patience. It will all work out. But, remember, the dough should be paper thin, or failing that, waxed-paper thin.
4. Fold each thin sheet of dough several times until you have a long roll. Then,

using a very sharp knife, cut the roll crossways into whatever width you desire. The Italians have a different name for every width.

5. Very gently unfold the strips and cut them into whatever lengths you desire. Dry the pasta on a board sprinkled with cornmeal for 1 hour.

Note: If you have a pasta machine, directions for its use should come in copious detail with the machine. However, patience is also required for kneading dough with the machine; you can't rush it. Each sheet of dough must be sent through the rollers at least three times on each setting, until it is 1/16" thick. Or thin. Thinness is all-important, otherwise the end product will be doughy.

SALSA PUTTANESCA

Ruth Spear

About 4 cups

Translated variously as "harlot's sauce" or "whore's sauce," this pasta sauce was presumably created by Italian prostitutes because it could be made very quickly between jobs!

2 TABLESPOONS OLIVE OIL
2 CLOVES GARLIC, MINCED
8 ANCHOVIES, CUT INTO PIECES
1 CAN (4½ CUPS) ITALIAN PLUM TOMATOES, PUT THROUGH A FOOD MILL OR A COARSE SIEVE
8 PITTED BLACK OLIVES, SLICED
1 TEASPOON CAPERS
1 TEASPOON DRIED SWEET BASIL OR 1 TABLESPOON CHOPPED FRESH BASIL
¼ TEASPOON CRUMBLED HOT RED PEPPER

1. In a skillet, heat the oil and sauté the garlic until soft. Then add the anchovies.
2. When the anchovies have broken apart, add the tomatoes and simmer for 10 minutes.
3. Stir in the olives, capers, basil and red pepper. Simmer, uncovered, for 20 minutes, or until the sauce has thickened.
4. Serve on *linguine* or *spaghettini*.

MACCHERONI ALLA CHITARRA

Giuliano Bugialli

6 servings

One traditional, time-honored method of making thin, even strands of pasta is with a special device called a *chitarra*; *chitarra* in Italian means guitar, and the device is so named because it looks like a stringed instrument. The pasta strands are formed when a sheet of dough is pressed through the *chitarra's* cutting wires.

Sauce:
¾ POUND LAMB SHOULDER
1 SCANT TABLESPOON SALT
½ TEASPOON FRESHLY GROUND BLACK PEPPER
6 TABLESPOONS OLIVE OIL
2 MEDIUM-SIZED CLOVES GARLIC, PEELED
2 BAY LEAVES
¾ CUP DRY WHITE WINE
1 CUP IMPORTED ITALIAN CANNED TOMATOES
2 GREEN PEPPERS

Pasta:
4 CUPS UNBLEACHED ALL-PURPOSE FLOUR
4 EGGS
4 TEASPOONS OLIVE OIL
PINCH OF SALT

1. With a pair of scissors, snip the lamb meat from the bone in small pieces (about ½" square). Place in a small bowl, add the salt and pepper and mix thoroughly with a wooden spoon.
2. In a medium-sized saucepan, preferably made of terra-cotta or enameled metal, heat the olive oil over medium flame. When the oil is warm, add the whole garlic cloves and whole bay leaves. Sauté very lightly for 2 minutes.
3. Then add the lamb, raise the heat and sauté for about 15 minutes, mixing every so often with a wooden spoon.
4. Add the wine, lower the heat, cover the pan with a lid and simmer for about 15 minutes to let the wine evaporate.
5. Add the tomatoes and cook, uncovered, for 10 minutes longer.
6. Remove the stem and seeds from the peppers and cut them into long thin strips. Add the peppers to the pan, cover again and let simmer for 1 hour, stirring occasionally. If the sauce gets too thick, add ¼ cup of hot broth or water.
7. Meanwhile, make the pasta dough. Combine all of the ingredients, mixing and kneading to form a smooth dough. Roll the dough into $^{1}/_{16}$"-thick sheets the size of the *chitarra*. Lay a sheet of dough over the *chitarra* strings and press it through with a rolling pin or your fingers to form the *maccheroni*. Repeat with the remaining sheets of dough. Place the *maccheroni* on a floured cotton towel to dry for 10 or 15 minutes.
8. Cook the pasta in a large quantity of boiling, salted water until *al dente*, for about 1 minute.
9. Strain the pasta and place it in a serving dish. Remove the bay leaves from the sauce and pour over the pasta. Serve immediately. Do *not* add cheese.

FRESH HERB PASTA

Mireille Johnston

6 servings

This is a delicious pasta. The addition of fragrant fresh herbs—mint, basil, chives, thin scallions, Italian parsley—to the dough gives a lively flavor to the noodles. The dish can be served as a main course with a little olive oil and some grated cheese. Sauces should not be used, as they would smother the fragrance of the herbs.

1 TO 2 CUPS MINCED FRESH HERBS (CHOOSE ONE OR TWO: MINT, BASIL, CHIVES, VERY SMALL SCALLIONS, ITALIAN PARSLEY)
4 CUPS UNBLEACHED FLOUR
6 EGGS, LIGHTLY BEATEN
SALT
4 TABLESPOONS OLIVE OIL
1 TEASPOON PEANUT OIL
FRESHLY GRATED PARMESAN OR SWISS CHEESE (OPTIONAL)

1. Dry the minced herbs thoroughly in a paper towel. If you prefer a paste, pound the herbs in a mortar.
2. Place the flour in a large bowl. Make a well in the center. Add the eggs, 1 tablespoon of salt, and 2 tablespoons of the olive oil and gradually work the flour into the eggs, mixing well.
3. Add the herbs, place on a counter or table and knead for about 20 minutes. Flour your hands and the work surface as often as necessary to prevent the dough from sticking. Keep pushing the dough away from you with the heel of your hand and gathering it back into a mass, until it is smooth and elastic. Make a ball of the dough, cover with a towel and let it rest for 1 hour.
4. Divide the ball into three parts. Roll each part through a pasta machine, following the manufacturer's instructions, to make thin sheets. Let the sheets of dough rest on a floured surface for 30 minutes, then pass them through the machine's cutting rollers to cut them into strips. Let them fall loosely on a floured tray. Sprinkle with flour.
5. Add salt and the peanut oil to a large pot filled about three-quarters full with water and bring to a boil. Add the pasta and cook, uncovered, for 5 to 10 minutes, depending on how tender you want it to be. Drain the pasta well.
6. Pour the drained pasta into a large bowl, add the remaining 2 tablespoons of olive oil, and toss with two forks.
7. Serve with a bowl of cheese, if desired.

MEAT-FILLED CANNELLONI WITH TOMATO SAUCE

Paul Rubinstein

6 servings

3½ CUPS ALL-PURPOSE FLOUR
7 EGGS
4 TABLESPOONS OLIVE OIL
¾ CUP DICED CARROT
½ CUP FINELY CHOPPED CELERY
½ CUP FINELY CHOPPED ONION
3 CUPS DICED FRESH TOMATOES
4 TABLESPOONS TOMATO PASTE
2 CUPS BEEF BROTH OR BOUILLON
1 BAY LEAF
½ TEASPOON FRESHLY GROUND BLACK PEPPER
½ TEASPOON SALT
6 TABLESPOONS (¾ STICK) BUTTER
2 CUPS HALF-AND-HALF OR 1 CUP CREAM, 1 CUP MILK
2 TABLESPOONS WORCESTERSHIRE SAUCE
1½ POUNDS FRESHLY GROUND CHUCK OR ROUND STEAK
¼ TEASPOON GROUND THYME
½ TEASPOON GARLIC SALT
1 CUP GRATED PARMESAN OR ROMANO CHEESE

1. Into a large mixing bowl, sift 3 cups of the flour. Then add 5 of the eggs, mix and knead by hand until the dough can be gathered into a mass. Transfer the dough to a pastry board and knead it to achieve a smooth and stiff consistency.
2. Divide the dough into three or four portions (depending on the size of the work surface available). With a lightly floured rolling pin, roll out each portion of dough as thin as possible without tearing it. Trim it into a 4''-wide, 6''-long strip. Add any leftover scraps to the next portion. Repeat until all of the dough has been used.
3. In a large stockpot, bring 4 to 6 quarts of water to a boil. Drop 4 or 5 dough strips into the water at a time. Boil for exactly 8 minutes, remove from the water with slotted spoons and spread the cooked strips between two damp towels.

   Note: When removing the cooked dough from the water, exercise great care because it is very slippery. A handy implement for this is a wide, flat, perforated spatula or a perforated, skimmer-type shallow ladle.
4. In a 2- to 3-quart saucepan, heat the olive oil and add the carrot, celery and onion. Cook over medium heat until the onion becomes soft and translucent.
5. Quickly stir in ¼ cup of the remaining flour, blend well, and continue to cook until the flour browns slightly.
6. Add the tomatoes, tomato paste, beef broth (or bouillon), bay leaf, ¼ teaspoon of the pepper and the salt and bring to a gentle simmer. Simmer 45 minutes, uncovered, stirring occasionally, until the sauce thickens.
7. Rub the sauce through a strainer and set it aside.
8. In a saucepan, melt 4 tablespoons of the butter over medium heat, add the last ¼ cup of flour, stir into a paste and cook for 2 minutes.
9. Add the half-and-half and continue stirring until the sauce thickens; then stir in the Worcestershire sauce and remove from the heat.
10. In a skillet, heat the remaining 2 tablespoons of butter. Add the ground beef and thyme and stir over medium heat until the meat has browned slightly.

11. Beat the remaining 2 eggs into the cream sauce, then beat the combination into the ground meat. Stir in the garlic salt, ¼ teaspoon pepper and ½ cup of the grated cheese and remove from the heat.
12. Preheat the oven to 375 F.
13. To assemble the *cannelloni*, spoon enough tomato sauce over the bottom of a deep, rectangular, ovenproof glass baking dish to cover it lightly. (Use more than one dish if a single large one is not available.)
14. Uncover the dough strips. Spoon 2 to 4 tablespoons of meat filling (depending on the thickness desired) onto each strip, roll up and place the rolls seam down in the baking dish, side by side. When the first layer is completed, spoon a thin layer of tomato sauce over it, sprinkle with Parmesan, then make the next layer.

    Note: Experiment with the amount of filling for each roll. The thickness of the dough will affect your decision, because it will have limited the number of pieces you have.
15. When the baking dish is well filled, top it with the remaining tomato sauce and Parmesan and bake for 25 minutes in the preheated oven.
16. Serve directly from the baking dish, which should be brought to the table and placed on a trivet. *Cannelloni* will stay quite hot for a while. Serve with a light green salad, crusty bread or garlic bread and a light Italian chianti or other red wine.

POTATO GNOCCHI

Mireille Johnston

6 servings

Technically more dumpling than pasta, *gnocchi* are nonetheless placed in the same category by the French and Italians. They are versatile enough to be sauced in a variety of ways—just like pasta.

5 MEDIUM-SIZED (ABOUT 2 POUNDS) BAKING POTATOES
2 EGG YOLKS
4 TABLESPOONS (½ STICK) BUTTER
½ TO 1 TEASPOON FRESHLY GRATED NUTMEG
2 TEASPOONS SALT
FRESHLY GROUND WHITE PEPPER, TO TASTE
1½ CUPS FLOUR
1 TABLESPOON PEANUT OIL
3 TABLESPOONS OLIVE OIL
SAUCE*
FRESHLY GRATED PARMESAN OR SWISS CHEESE
3 TABLESPOONS FINELY MINCED CHIVES, MINT OR BASIL

1. Scrub the potatoes and cook them in boiling, salted water until they are tender. Protect your hands by using a kitchen towel or an oven mitt, and peel them while they are still hot. Put them immediately through a food mill (do not use a blender because it will turn them into a sticky paste).
2. Slowly beat in the egg yolks, butter, nutmeg, salt and pepper. Taste for salt and

Continued from preceding page

add more, if desired.

3. Add the flour gradually, beating with a wooden spoon or an electric mixer. The finished dough should be soft and smooth, but not too sticky; add more flour if it is too moist.
4. Dust your hands with flour and divide the dough into balls the size of small apples. Roll each one out to a cylindrical shape about ½'' in diameter, then cut it into pieces about ½'' long.
5. Cover the *gnocchi* with a towel and keep in the refrigerator or at room temperature for a few hours.

   Note: The dish can be prepared in advance up to this point.
6. Bring a kettle of salted water to a boil. Add the *gnocchi* and the peanut oil. Cook them for 7 to 10 minutes, or until all have floated to the surface. They should be elastic to the touch.
7. Drain well and place in a warm, shallow dish. Sprinkle with the olive oil and stir gently, then add your favorite sauce and the cheese. Sprinkle with the chives, mint or basil just before serving.

Note: The *gnocchi* can also be made to resemble shells—they not only will look prettier, but will absorb the sauce better. To make the shells, press each of the pieces of uncooked dough down against the tines of a fork and roll it off the end of the fork with your thumb.

* *Gnocchi* take well to many sauces, including *pistou*, and they are delicious with a roast, especially if you deglaze the pan with white wine.

FETTUCCINE IN CLAM BROTH

Eliza and Joshua Baer

4 to 5 first course servings/3 main course servings

We invented this recipe to serve as an entrée at Cafe Figaro in Carmel, California.

24 FRESH CHERRYSTONE CLAMS*
8 TABLESPOONS (1 STICK) BUTTER
3 CLOVES GARLIC, PEELED
¾ TO 1¼ CUPS DRY VERMOUTH
1 POUND DRY OR FRESH *FETTUCCINE*
2 TABLESPOONS CHOPPED PARSLEY
¾ CUP FRESHLY GRATED PARMESAN
1 LEMON, SLICED

1. Wash the clams in cold water, rinsing them of any sand or water. Set them aside in a strainer.
2. Fill a large pot three-quarters full of water and place it over high heat. (This is

to be used for cooking the *fettuccine*. If the water comes to a boil before you reach Step 7, add 2 or 3 more cups of cold water and let the water come to a second boil.)

3. In a large frying pan, melt 2 tablespoons of butter. When it begins to foam, toss in the 3 whole cloves of garlic.
4. Dump the 24 clams into the pan. Stir them around with a wooden spoon to coat the shells with butter.

   Note: This makes the clam shells smooth and glossy when served.
5. Add ¾ cup of vermouth to the pan and bring it to a simmer. When the alcohol starts to evaporate, cover the pan and turn the heat down to medium low.
6. The clams will take 5 to 10 minutes to open. When most of them have opened (1 or 2 out of each dozen will open stubbornly), turn off the heat and let the pan sit while proceeding with the recipe.

   Note: Check the clams frequently during Steps 4, 5 and 6. If the level of vermouth gets low, add another ½ cup.
7. Cook the *fettuccine* in the large pot of boiling water until *al dente*. Drain the *fettuccine* and then spill it into a large, warm bowl.
8. Add the remaining 6 tablespoons of butter, the chopped parsley and the Parmesan and toss the *fettuccine* like a salad for 20 to 30 seconds but do not let it cool.
9. Turn on the heat under the clams.
10. Transfer portions of the *fettuccine* from the large bowl to individual serving bowls. (Use wide, shallow bowls with rims.)
11. As soon as the clam broth begins to simmer, remove the pan from the heat. Arrange 8 clams around the edge of each bowl of *fettuccine* for main course servings, 5 to 6 per bowl for first course servings.
12. Then, using a ladle or a large spoon, spoon small amounts of the clam broth into each opened clam, and pour the remaining broth over each portion of *fettuccine*.

    Note: The broth has a very pronounced flavor. If you want a milder broth, use either white wine instead of vermouth or a combination of water and vermouth.
13. Arrange 2 or 3 slices of lemon among the clams in each bowl, and serve immediately with hot French bread and plenty of butter.

* If you really like clams, increase the number of clams to 10 to 12 per person, but be sure to double the amounts of butter and vermouth used to cook them.

FETTUCCINE WITH TOMATO, MUSHROOMS, ZUCCHINI AND CLAM SAUCE

Paula Buchholz

6 servings

2 CUPS SLICED FRESH MUSHROOMS
1 MEDIUM-SIZED ZUCCHINI, SHREDDED
8 TABLESPOONS (1 STICK) BUTTER
1 TOMATO, PEELED AND DICED
1 POUND FRESH *FETTUCCINE*
1½ CUPS FRESHLY GRATED PARMESAN
1 CUP HEAVY CREAM
1 CAN (10 OUNCES) BABY CLAMS, UNDRAINED

1. Sauté the mushrooms and zucchini in 4 tablespoons of the butter for a few minutes.
2. Gently stir in the tomato and keep warm.
3. Cook the *fettuccine* in boiling, salted water until tender, but still *al dente*.
4. Drain the *fettuccine* and return it to the pan along with the remaining 4 tablespoons butter, the cheese and cream. With two forks, gently toss the pasta until the cheese melts and the sauce coats the pasta, then stir in the clams and vegetables.
5. Serve immediately on warm plates. Accompany the *fettuccine* with a Bibb lettuce salad (dressed lightly in lemon juice and olive oil), crusty sourdough bread and dry white wine.

SPAGHETTI WITH ANCHOVY PASTE

Eliza and Joshua Baer

4 first course servings/2 main course servings

We developed this recipe as a speedy alternative to *pesto genovese*. Anchovy paste (available in tubes at most supermarkets) keeps indefinitely; and keeping garlic, parsley and Parmesan cheese on hand is easier than maintaining a steady supply of fresh basil and pine nuts.

8 TABLESPOONS (1 STICK) BUTTER
¼ CUP OLIVE OIL
5 TO 6 CLOVES GARLIC, CRUSHED OR FINELY CHOPPED
½ CUP CHOPPED FRESH PARSLEY
1 TO 1½ TABLESPOONS ANCHOVY PASTE

SALT, TO TASTE
FRESHLY GROUND BLACK PEPPER, TO TASTE
¾ POUND SPAGHETTI
FRESHLY GRATED PARMESAN

1. In a frying pan, heat the butter and oil. When the butter foams, add the garlic and take the pan off the heat. The garlic should cook slowly and soften. Do not let it brown, or burn.
2. Mix half of the parsley with the softened garlic, then add the anchovy paste. Mix everything well over very low heat for 1 or 2 minutes. Do not let the garlic brown. Season with salt and pepper, then cover the mixture and set it aside, off the heat.
3. Cook the spaghetti *al dente*, drain and put it in a large glass bowl.
4. Cook the sauce mixture over high heat for 30 seconds, then pour it on top of the spaghetti. Add the rest of the chopped parsley to the spaghetti while tossing it like a salad.
5. Serve the spaghetti on white plates. Sprinkle generous amounts of grated Parmesan cheese over each serving. This is an excellent pasta to serve before veal or lamb.

Note: Try to have the garlic/anchovy paste/parsley mixture ready when the spaghetti is done so there will be no loss of heat. Increase the amount of anchovy paste for a stronger, more unusual flavor. If the spaghetti tastes too strong, use less garlic the next time.

SUMMER SPAGHETTI WITH OLIVES

Jane Moulton

6 servings

In the middle of summer, when zucchini squash abounds, it is likely to turn up in almost anything. It adds color, flavor and an interesting texture, but very few calories, to a spaghetti sauce.

1 POUND LEAN GROUND BEEF
3 MEDIUM-SIZED ONIONS, COARSELY CHOPPED
1 CLOVE GARLIC, PEELED AND PUT THROUGH A PRESS OR CRUSHED
2 POUNDS ZUCCHINI, THINLY SLICED*
2 TEASPOONS SALT
2 TEASPOONS DRIED BASIL
2 TEASPOONS DRIED OREGANO
½ TEASPOON SUGAR
½ TEASPOON FENNEL SEEDS (OPTIONAL)
½ CUP PIMIENTO-STUFFED OLIVES, CUT UP, PLUS RESERVED JUICE
1 CAN (ABOUT 15 OUNCES) TOMATO PURÉE
½ POUND SPAGHETTI, COOKED
PARMESAN, GRATED

1. In a heavy 11" or 12" skillet, start to brown the ground beef over medium heat, breaking up the meat with a wooden spoon. Add the onion and garlic just as the meat begins to brown and sauté until the onion turns translucent and the meat is brown. Spoon off the excess fat.

Continued from preceding page

2. Add the zucchini and sprinkle with the salt, basil, oregano, sugar, fennel seeds (if you are using them) and the olives. Toss with two spoons to mix well.
3. Add the tomato purée and ¼ cup of the reserved olive juice; mix well. Cover and simmer for 10 minutes. Remove the cover and simmer until the consistency of a proper spaghetti sauce is reached, about 20 minutes.
4. Serve over cooked spaghetti. Pass grated Parmesan cheese, separately, and accompany with sweet corn, green salad and sesame bread sticks.

* Young, tender zucchini may be used without peeling or seeding. With over-developed zucchini, peel and seed before slicing (although the pretty green color and texture of the skin will be lost) and use about 2½ pounds to compensate for the loss of skin and seeds.

FUSILLI WITH PESTO

Nicola Zanghi

4 servings

In Genoa, pasta with *pesto* (basil and garlic sauce) is always served with potatoes and green beans. The pasta is cooked in the same water used to cook the potatoes and beans, thereby giving the pasta itself more flavor. This extremely popular summer pasta dish may be served as a luncheon main course, a first course preceding cold meat or fish, and the sauce alone is excellent with cold meat or fish.

***Pesto**:**

2 CLOVES GARLIC
5 BUNCHES (ABOUT 4 CUPS, PACKED) FRESH BASIL, WELL WASHED
4 TABLESPOONS PINE NUTS, TOASTED
8 TABLESPOONS GRATED PARMESAN
8 SPRIGS PARSLEY
1 TEASPOON SALT
10 GRINDS OF PEPPER
1 CUP OLIVE OIL

Pasta:

4 TO 6 SMALL TO MEDIUM-SIZED POTATOES, SCRUBBED BUT UNPEELED
2 TABLESPOONS SALT
¼ POUND FRESH STRING BEANS
1 POUND *FUSILLI* OR OTHER CURLY PASTA
4 TABLESPOONS (½ STICK) LIGHTLY SALTED BUTTER, MELTED

1. Using a blender, food processor or mortar and pestle, blend together all of the *pesto* ingredients, adding just enough oil to obtain a proper sauce consistency.
2. In a large saucepot, boil the potatoes in water with 2 tablespoons of salt for about 12 to 15 minutes.
3. Add the beans and cook 5 minutes longer.
4. Pour the water and vegetables through a colander set over a large pot or bowl to retain the cooking water.

5. Return the water to a rolling boil and add the pasta, stirring frequently so the noodles do not stick. Cook until *al dente*, or about 5 minutes.
6. Meanwhile, peel and slice the potatoes; keep warm.
7. Drain the pasta, transfer it to a serving platter, add the butter and mix thoroughly.
8. Arrange the potatoes and beans around the circumference of the plate and generously spoon the *pesto* over the pasta.

* *Pesto* can be kept indefinitely if only the parsley and basil are blended; add the remaining ingredients before serving.

SICILIAN FETTUCCINE

Alma Lach

6 servings

1 PACKAGE (8 OUNCES) *FETTUCCINE*
SALT
6 TABLESPOONS (¾ STICK) BUTTER
1 MEDIUM-SIZED CLOVE GARLIC, MINCED
2 SHALLOTS, MINCED
1 GREEN ONION, SLICED (INCLUDING 1" OF THE GREEN PART)
FRESHLY GROUND PEPPER
3 LARGE EGGS
½ CUP GRATED PARMESAN

1. Cook the noodles in lots of boiling water seasoned with salt and 2 tablespoons of butter.
2. Meanwhile, sauté the garlic, shallots and onion in the remaining 4 tablespoons of butter for about 2 minutes. Remove from the heat. Add ½ teaspoon of salt and more pepper than you think you will like.
3. Break the eggs into a very large mixing bowl. Whip them with a whisk until light.
4. Drain the noodles in a colander and run very hot tap water over them. Drain them again and pour back into the pot. Dry them off over low heat for a few seconds.
5. Pour the warm butter-garlic mixture into the eggs and mix. Add a few hot noodles and toss with a salad spoon and fork. Add more noodles and toss. Add the balance of the noodles and toss. The eggs should begin to coat the noodles. Add the cheese and toss and serve immediately.

Note: The trick of this recipe is that the hot noodles must not cook the eggs. If they do, the eggs will curdle, and neither the taste nor looks will be right. Prepare the dish at the very last moment and serve promptly.

SPAGHETTI WITH GENOESE HERBAL OIL

Paula Wolfert

8 servings

¼ CUP CHOPPED FRESH PARSLEY
¼ CUP CHOPPED FRESH BASIL
¼ CUP CHOPPED FRESH OR 2 TABLESPOONS DRIED TARRAGON
2 TABLESPOONS CHOPPED ROSEMARY
2 TABLESPOONS DRIED SAGE LEAVES
1 TEASPOON DRIED MARJORAM OR OREGANO
1 TEASPOON FENNEL SEEDS
2 CRUMBLED BAY LEAVES
2 DRIED HOT RED PEPPERS, CRUSHED
1 CUP FRUITY OLIVE OIL
SALT, TO TASTE
1½ POUNDS SPAGHETTI
1 CUP GRATED PARMESAN

1. In a mixing bowl, combine the herbs and the red peppers, and cover them with the olive oil. Stir, pressing down on the herbs. Let the mixture stand for 12 hours or more.
2. Press the herbal oil through the finest disk of a food mill; the oil should be a deep green color and very aromatic. Discard the herbs. Add salt and blend it in.
3. In a large pot of boiling, salted water, cook the spaghetti *al dente*.
4. In a saucepan, heat the herbal oil being careful not to let it boil.
5. Drain the spaghetti, toss it with the oil and serve at once with plenty of grated Parmesan cheese.

BAKED PENNE WITH EGGPLANT AND CHEESE

Maria Luisa Scott and Jack Denton Scott

6 servings

12 SLICES PEELED EGGPLANT, EACH 2½" IN DIAMETER
SALT, TO TASTE
PEPPER, TO TASTE
FLOUR
1 CUP PLUS 2 TABLESPOONS OLIVE OIL
3 MEDIUM-SIZED WHITE ONIONS, CHOPPED
2 CUPS HOMEMADE TOMATO SAUCE OR 2 CANS (8 OUNCES EACH) COMMERCIAL SAUCE
2 TABLESPOONS CHOPPED ITALIAN PARSLEY
2 TABLESPOONS CHOPPED FRESH BASIL OR 1 TEASPOON DRIED BASIL
1 POUND *PENNE* (PASTA TUBES)
3 TABLESPOONS BUTTER
1 CUP GRATED *ASIAGO* OR PARMESAN CHEESE
12 THIN SLICES MOZZARELLA CHEESE

1. Preheat the oven to 375 F.
2. Season the eggplant slices with salt and pepper and dredge them with flour.
3. In a large frying pan, heat 1 cup of the oil and brown the eggplant slices; drain them on paper towels.

4. In a saucepan, heat the 2 tablespoons of oil. Add the onion and cook it until soft. Stir in the tomato sauce, parsley and basil and season with salt and pepper. Heat thoroughly and keep warm.
5. Cook the *penne* in 5 quarts of salted, boiling water until *al dente*. Drain.
6. In a large, warm bowl, place the hot, drained pasta and toss it with the butter.
7. Pour half of the tomato sauce into the pasta bowl and gently toss, blending well.
8. Butter a casserole or baking dish and add a layer of *penne*, then one of eggplant, then a sprinkling of the grated cheese, and repeat layering until the ingredients are used up.
9. Cover the last layer with the remaining tomato sauce and arrange the mozzarella cheese in a layer on top.
10. Bake, uncovered, in the preheated oven until the cheese has melted and the sauce is bubbling.

LINGUE DI PASSERI PICCOLE WITH ANCHOVIES AND ARTICHOKES

Maria Luisa Scott and Jack Denton Scott

6 servings

½ CUP OLIVE OIL
2 CLOVES GARLIC, PEELED AND CRUSHED, PLUS 2 CLOVES GARLIC, PEELED
2 CANS (2 OUNCES EACH) FLAT ANCHOVIES, DICED, OIL RESERVED
1/8 TEASPOON HOT RED PEPPER FLAKES
2 TABLESPOONS CHOPPED ITALIAN PARSLEY
5 ARTICHOKE HEARTS (CANNED, FRESH COOKED OR FROZEN), COARSELY CHOPPED
1 POUND *LINGUE DI PASSERI PICCOLE* (A THINNER TYPE OF *LINGUINE*)
4 TABLESPOONS (½ STICK) BUTTER

1. In a saucepan, heat the oil. Add the 2 crushed garlic cloves and cook them over medium heat until brown; remove and discard.
2. Lower the heat and force the 2 whole garlic cloves through a garlic press into the hot oil. Stir in the anchovies and their oil and cook for 1 minute.
3. Add the pepper flakes, parsley and artichoke hearts; cook 3 minutes.
4. Cook the pasta in 5 quarts of salted, boiling water until *al dente*. Drain.
5. Place the drained, hot pasta in a hot bowl, add the butter and gently toss.
6. To prevent the pasta from getting gummy, add one-third of the anchovy-artichoke sauce and toss to blend. Repeat with another third of the sauce. Save the last third of the sauce to spoon on top of individual servings.

FETTUCCINE WITH SEA DELIGHTS (FETTUCCINE AL FRUTTI DI MARE)

Nicola Zanghi

4 servings

⅔ CUP OLIVE OIL
4 TABLESPOONS (½ STICK) BUTTER, MELTED
⅓ CUP DICED SCALLION (WHITE PART ONLY)
1 CLOVE GARLIC, MINCED
½ POUND MEDIUM-SIZED SHRIMP, PEELED AND DEVEINED
½ POUND BAY SCALLOPS
20 TO 24 LITTLENECK CLAMS, WELL WASHED
⅔ CUP DRY WHITE WINE
1 CUP PEELED, PURÉED* PLUM TOMATOES
PINCH OF OREGANO
PINCH OF BASIL
PINCH OF CRUSHED HOT RED PEPPER FLAKES
1 TEASPOON CHOPPED PARSLEY
2 TABLESPOONS BRANDY
1 POUND *FETTUCCINE*

1. In a saucepan over medium heat, combine ⅓ cup of the olive oil and the butter. Add the scallion and sauté until limp. Add the garlic, sauté 1 minute. Add the shrimp, sauté 2 minutes. Add the scallops, sauté 2 minutes. Add the clams and wine and boil for 3 minutes. Finally, add the tomatoes, seasonings and brandy. Cover and let simmer for 3 to 5 minutes, or until the clams open.
2. Meanwhile, boil the *fettuccine* in rapidly boiling, salted water until *al dente*, or firm, about 5 minutes. Drain, transfer to a serving platter and mix thoroughly with the remaining ⅓ cup of olive oil.

   Note: All pasta should be cooked in large, 6- to 10-quart pots. The pasta should be stirred, lifted out of the water and shaken off the tines of a fork to be sure that it will not stick. Coating it with butter or oil before saucing guarantees non-stick pasta.
3. Arrange the open clams around the circumference of the platter and spoon the remaining sauce in the center.

* Purée the tomatoes through a food mill so they retain some texture.

LINGUINE WITH WHITE CLAM SAUCE

Maria Luisa Scott and Jack Denton Scott

6 servings

We have experimented for months with this white clam sauce, as the dish is among our favorites. No matter how careful we were, fresh clams always came out chewy or, sometimes, downright tough. Then we went to canned clams, coupled with virtually an essence-of-clam sauce, which packed plenty of authority and yet had a supremely delicate flavor. Sometimes we dress the individual plates of pasta with 3 or 4 cherrystone clams, lightly steamed *just* until they open. They give an authentic touch of the sea that is greatly appreciated.

3 TABLESPOONS OLIVE OIL
3 CLOVES GARLIC, PEELED AND CRUSHED, PLUS 3 CLOVES GARLIC, PEELED
4 BOTTLES (8 OUNCES EACH) CLAM BROTH
2 CANS (8 OUNCES EACH) MINCED CLAMS, DRAINED, LIQUID RESERVED
1 CAN (10 OUNCES) WHOLE BABY CLAMS, DRAINED, LIQUID RESERVED
¾ CUP DRY WHITE WINE
¼ TEASPOON HOT RED PEPPER FLAKES
SALT
1 POUND *LINGUINE*
3 TABLESPOONS BUTTER
3 TABLESPOONS CHOPPED ITALIAN PARSLEY
18 TO 24 SMALL CHERRYSTONE CLAMS (OPTIONAL)

1. In a deep saucepan, heat the oil. Add the crushed garlic cloves and cook over medium heat until the garlic is brown. Discard the garlic.
2. Remove the pan from the heat. Force the remaining garlic cloves through a garlic press into the hot oil and pour in the clam broth, the liquid from the canned clams, the wine, red pepper flakes and a gentle shake of salt. (Although clam broth is salty, a little extra salt is needed.) Cook over medium heat, uncovered, for 10 minutes.
3. Lower the heat and cook, stirring frequently, for 25 minutes, or until the sauce has reduced to about one-third of its original volume.
4. Meanwhile, cook the pasta in 5 quarts of salted, boiling water until just *al dente*. Drain.
5. Place the hot, drained pasta in a large, warm bowl, add the butter and parsley and toss gently but well.
6. Stir the drained minced and whole baby clams into the clam sauce, blending well. Bring to a simmer. Immediately remove from the heat.
7. Spoon half of the sauce (with some of the clams) into the pasta bowl and toss.
8. Serve the pasta in hot plates, spooning the remaining sauce on top. If you like, dress each plate with 3 or 4 small cherrystone clams, cooked just until the shells open.

LINGUINE WITH FRESH TOMATO-PESTO SAUCE

Emanuel and Madeline Greenberg

3 to 4 servings

Another name for this dish could be "*Linguine*-End-Of-Summer." That's when the tomatoes are ripe and flavorful and fresh basil is at its peak. Note that the pasta is hot and the uncooked sauce is at room temperature.

⅓ CUP OLIVE OIL
1 CUP FRESH BASIL LEAVES
2 TABLESPOONS CHOPPED WALNUTS
2 CLOVES GARLIC, PEELED AND CRUSHED

Continued from preceding page

⅓ CUP GRATED PARMESAN PLUS
ABOUT ¼ CUP GRATED PARMESAN
½ TEASPOON SALT, OR TO TASTE
GRIND OF PEPPER
1 POUND (ABOUT 3 MEDIUM-SIZED)
RIPE TOMATOES, PEELED
1 POUND *LINGUINE*

1. Pour the olive oil into a blender container. Add the basil leaves, walnuts and garlic and whirl until smoothly blended.
2. Transfer the basil mixture to a bowl and stir in ⅓ cup of the grated Parmesan and the salt and pepper.
3. Place a large strainer over the bowl. Cut the peeled tomatoes in half over the strainer so that the juice goes into the bowl. Scoop the seeds out of the tomatoes into the strainer and push through all the juices and bits of tomato pulp. Discard the seeds.
4. Remove the strainer, cut the tomatoes in small chunks and add them to the basil sauce. Stir the sauce gently and let it stand at room temperature while you prepare the *linguine*.
5. Cook the *linguine* in boiling, salted water according to the directions on the package.
6. Drain the *linguine* well and turn it into a large, warmed bowl. Add the sauce and stir gently to distribute it through the pasta. Serve with additional grated Parmesan, and pass the pepper mill.

Note: *Fettuccine* is a good substitute for the *linguine*.

SPAGHETTI WITH EGGPLANT AND SAUSAGE

Nan Mabon

5 servings

I had a pasta dish like this in Rome several years ago. The difficulty was in locating a sausage in this country that came close in flavor to the one in Italy. I have finally decided that Polish sausage comes closest to the taste I remember.

1 EGGPLANT, ABOUT 1 POUND
SALT
1 POUND SOFT, SMOKED, GARLIC-FLAVORED POLISH SAUSAGE
12 TABLESPOONS (1½ STICKS) BUTTER, MELTED
2 CLOVES GARLIC, PEELED AND FINELY MINCED

1 POUND SPAGHETTI
¾ CUP FRESHLY GRATED PARMESAN
FRESHLY GROUND BLACK PEPPER

1. Cube the eggplant, leaving the skin on, then sprinkle with salt. Let drain in a colander for an hour, then rinse with water and pat dry with paper towels.

   Note: This step is essential. The eggplant will be bitter if it is not salted and drained before cooking.
2. Remove the sausage casing and cut the meat into ½" cubes.
3. In a large pot, place 6 quarts of salted water and bring it to a boil.
4. Meanwhile, in a large frying pan, heat 3 tablespoons of the melted butter and fry the eggplant, stirring constantly, until almost tender. Add the garlic and cook for a minute, then add the sausage and heat through.
5. When the water is boiling, plunge the spaghetti into the pot. Cook until just tender, then drain.
6. In a large bowl, toss the steaming spaghetti with the eggplant-sausage mixture, the remaining 9 tablespoons of butter, the Parmesan cheese, salt and pepper to taste. Serve immediately. This can be served both as a main course or, in smaller portions, as a pasta course before the main course.

STUFFED PASTA WITH MEAT (AGNOLOTTI TOSCANI)

Paula Wolfert

6 first course servings

THREE 1½-OUNCE VEAL SCALLOPS
3 TABLESPOONS BUTTER
1 TEASPOON BEEF MARROW
4 OUNCES MORTADELLA SAUSAGE, FINELY CHOPPED
1 EGG, LIGHTLY BEATEN
GRATED PARMESAN
FRESHLY GRATED NUTMEG
SALT
FRESHLY GROUND BLACK PEPPER
1 POUND FRESHLY MADE HOMEMADE PASTA DOUGH
8 TABLESPOONS (1 STICK) BUTTER, MELTED

1. Sauté the veal in the butter until golden brown and cooked through. Remove the veal from the pan and allow to cool.
2. Add the marrow to the pan juices. Lower the heat and cook gently, mashing the marrow into the buttery juices. Scrape into a mixing bowl.
3. Finely chop the cooled veal, mix with the mortadella, and chop together until pasty. Add to the mixing bowl.

Continued from preceding page

4. Stir in the egg and 2 tablespoons of Parmesan. Season with nutmeg, salt and pepper to taste. Combine thoroughly.
5. Separate the dough into four portions. Roll out one portion into a thin sheet measuring 11" x 17".
6. Using a teaspoon, place small mounds of stuffing 2½" apart on the pasta sheet.
7. Roll out a second ball of dough to the same size. Cover the first sheet, and lightly press around each mound with your fingers.
8. Dip a 2"-round pasta cutter into flour and cut the filled sheets of dough into rounds. Press down firmly around the edges of each *agnolotti* to seal them securely.
9. Repeat with the last two portions of pasta dough. As the *agnolotti* are being made, line them up on a floured cloth and cover with a second cloth, to keep them from drying out. Let them sit for at least 30 minutes before cooking.

   Note: The *agnolotti* will keep, refrigerated and covered with a cloth, for up to 24 hours.
10. Drop the *agnolotti* into boiling, salted water and cook for 3 to 5 minutes, or until they rise to the surface. Test to see if they are tender.
11. Drain and serve at once with melted butter and grated Parmesan.

LASAGNE WITH FENNEL SAUSAGES

Nicola Zanghi

8 servings

Sauce:
¼ CUP OLIVE OIL
¼ CUP MINCED SHALLOTS (WHITE PART ONLY)
1 CLOVE GARLIC, MINCED
¼ POUND *PROSCIUTTO*, WESTPHALIAN OR OTHER COUNTRY-TYPE HAM, DICED
½ CUP DRIED OR 1 CUP SLICED FRESH MUSHROOMS
¼ CUP MARSALA
4 CUPS PEELED, COARSELY CHOPPED AND DRAINED PLUM TOMATOES
¼ TEASPOON OREGANO
½ TEASPOON DRIED OR 2 TABLESPOONS MINCED FRESH BASIL
½ TEASPOON FENNEL SEEDS
SALT
FRESHLY GROUND BLACK PEPPER

Other Ingredients:
¾ POUND FENNEL SAUSAGES
1 POUND PACKAGED OR FRESH LASAGNE
4 TABLESPOONS (½ STICK) BUTTER, MELTED
1 POUND RICOTTA CHEESE
½ POUND MOZZARELLA, CUT INTO ½" CUBES
1 CUP FRESHLY GRATED PARMESAN
FRESHLY GRATED NUTMEG
FRESHLY GROUND PEPPER

1. In a thick-bottomed saucepan, heat the olive oil and sauté the scallions over medium heat until limp. Add the garlic and sauté for 2 minutes. Add the *pros-*

ciutto (or country-type ham) and mushrooms and sauté for 5 more minutes. Add the Marsala. Let the mixture reduce for approximately 3 minutes.

2. Add the tomatoes, bring to a boil, then reduce the heat and simmer for 15 minutes.
3. Add the oregano, basil and fennel seeds. Taste for salt (you should need about ½ teaspoon) and season with 6 twists of the peppermill. Simmer for 5 more minutes. Reserve.
4. Prick the sausages, place in a saucepan with a little water and steam for 10 minutes. Remove, drain and, when cool, cut into ¼"-thick slices.
5. Boil the noodles in salted water until *al dente* or "resilient," about 5 minutes for commercial lasagne, less for fresh. Do *not* overcook.
6. With a slotted spoon, remove the noodles to a bowl of ice water. When cool, remove the noodles to a damp tablecloth and spread them out.
7. Preheat the oven to 375 F.
8. Brush a 4-quart baking or lasagne dish (at least 2" deep) with some of the melted butter.
9. Cover the bottom of the dish lengthwise with a layer of noodles. Lightly cover them with about one-quarter of the tomato sauce. Spread approximately one-third of the cheeses and sausage slices on top of the sauce. Lightly dust with nutmeg and pepper.
10. Cover with another layer of noodles, this time placed widthwise. Repeat the filling sequence with the sauce, cheeses, sausage and seasonings.
11. Make another lengthwise layer of noodles and repeat the filling steps.
12. Cover the casserole widthwise with the remaining noodles. Spread the remaining melted butter and tomato sauce on top, cover the casserole with a dampened towel and bake in the preheated oven for 45 minutes.

Note: Keep the towel moist throughout the baking to prevent the top layer of noodles from drying out. Lasagne may be frozen in an air-tight container either before or after cooking.

TORTELLINI COOKED IN CHICKEN BROTH

Paul Rubinstein

6 pasta servings/8 to 10 soup servings

This recipe is both for the preparation of *tortellini* (stuffed pasta rings) and for cooking the prepared rings in chicken broth for the extra flavor that it imparts to the pasta.

3 CUPS ALL-PURPOSE FLOUR
6 EGGS
8 TABLESPOONS (1 STICK) BUTTER
2 WHOLE CHICKEN BREASTS, SPLIT
2½ QUARTS CHICKEN BROTH OR BOUILLON
1¼ CUPS FRESH RICOTTA CHEESE
1 CUP GRATED PARMESAN
¼ CUP FINELY CHOPPED FRESH PARSLEY
½ TEASPOON SALT
¼ TEASPOON GROUND ALLSPICE

1. Into a large mixing bowl, sift the flour. Add 4 of the eggs, mix and then knead by hand until the dough can be gathered into a mass. Transfer to a pastry board and knead to form into a smooth and stiff dough.
2. Divide the dough into three or four portions (depending on the size of the surface available for rolling out). With a lightly floured rolling pin, roll out the dough into as thin a sheet as possible without tearing. Using a 2''-round cookie cutter or inverted glass or small can, cut the dough into circles. Lay the circles out on one or two damp towels and let them stand while the filling is prepared.
3. In a medium-sized skillet equipped with a cover, heat 3 tablespoons of butter. Add the split chicken breasts and sauté lightly for 3 minutes on each side.
4. Add 2 cups of the chicken broth, cover and simmer for 20 minutes, until cooked through.
5. Remove the breasts from the pan and allow them to cool a few minutes. Remove the skin and bones and run the meat through the finest blade of a meat grinder.
6. Beat the remaining 2 eggs and combine them in a mixing bowl with the ground chicken, ricotta, ½ cup of the Parmesan, the parsley, salt and allspice. Blend well by hand or with a wooden spoon.
7. In a large saucepan or stockpot, bring the remaining 2 quarts of chicken broth to a boil.
8. While the broth is heating, place about 1 teaspoon of filling on a circle of dough. Fold it over once to make a semi-circle and pinch the edges together. Then wrap the semi-circle around a finger so that the two points meet. Squeeze the points together so that they stick to one another. Set aside and repeat the process with each of the remaining circles.
9. Cook the finished *tortellini* in the boiling chicken broth for 15 minutes, or until the dough is cooked through but not gluey. Drain in a colander.

10. Transfer to a serving dish, dot with the remaining 5 tablespoons of butter, sprinkle on the remaining ½ cup of grated Parmesan and serve hot.

Note: The *tortellini* may also be served as a soup course. To do this, reserve the broth when the pasta is drained, then strain it to remove any stray bits of pasta. Spoon the broth into bowls and float the *tortellini* in it.

FETTUCCINE WITH TOMATO FILETS (FETTUCCINE AL FILETTO)

Nicola Zanghi

4 servings

A classic Italian dish that departs from the slow-cooked marinara or basic tomato sauce, *salsa filetto* is finished in 8 minutes. The bacon and *prosciutto* add a slightly smokey taste to the sauce.

½ CUP OLIVE OIL
½ CUP SLICED SCALLIONS (WHITE PART ONLY)
3 STRIPS BACON, DICED
¼ POUND *PROSCIUTTO*, CUT INTO JULIENNE STRIPS
2½ CUPS PEELED, QUARTERED, SEEDED AND JUICED PLUM TOMATOES*
½ TEASPOON OREGANO
1 TEASPOON DRIED OR 4 TO 6 LEAVES FRESH BASIL
1 TEASPOON CHOPPED FRESH PARSLEY
¼ TEASPOON CRUSHED HOT RED PEPPER FLAKES
1 POUND *FETTUCCINE*
4 TABLESPOONS (½ STICK) BUTTER, MELTED

1. In a saucepan over moderate heat, heat the olive oil and sauté the scallions until limp.
2. Add the bacon and allow it to soften, then add the *prosciutto* and sauté for 5 minutes.
3. Add the tomatoes and seasonings. Bring to a boil, then reduce the heat and simmer for 5 minutes.
4. Meanwhile, cook the *fettuccine* in rapidly boiling, salted water for 5 minutes, or until *al dente*.
5. Drain, transfer to a serving platter and mix thoroughly with the melted butter.
6. Spoon the sauce over the pasta. Follow with a hearty meat course.

Note: As with all pasta dishes, *filetto* must be served immediately.

* Fresh plum or pear-type tomatoes should be used when available. Otherwise, use imported, canned plum tomatoes.

COLD NOODLES ITALIAN

Nan Mabon

6 to 8 servings

The inspiration for this dish came from a Chinese recipe. In the Chinese version, the egg noodles are seasoned with soy, vinegar and sesame oil; then, everyone mixes his own salad from an assortment of ingredients that might include bean sprouts, roast pork and cabbage.

Dressing:
1 TABLESPOON DIJON MUSTARD
2 TABLESPOONS LEMON JUICE, FRESHLY SQUEEZED
SALT, TO TASTE
FRESHLY GROUND BLACK PEPPER, TO TASTE
5 TABLESPOONS OLIVE OIL
1 CLOVE GARLIC, CRUSHED

Other Ingredients:
1 POUND FRESH *FETTUCCINE* NOODLES OR ANY DRY PASTA
¼ POUND *PROSCIUTTO*, CUT INTO THIN STRIPS
¼ POUND GENOA SALAMI, CUT INTO THIN STRIPS
1 RIPE TOMATO, FINELY CHOPPED
¼ POUND OIL-CURED BLACK OLIVES, PITTED AND CUT IN HALF
1 BUNCH SCALLIONS, FINELY CHOPPED
1 MEDIUM-SIZED ZUCCHINI, FINELY CHOPPED

1. Prepare the dressing: Blend together the mustard, lemon juice, salt and pepper; slowly whisk in the olive oil, then stir in the garlic.
2. Plunge the noodles into a large pot of boiling, salted water and cook until *al dente*, just tender. Drain and toss the noodles in the dressing.
3. Allow the noodles to sit for about 30 minutes in the dressing and serve at room temperature. Place all the remaining ingredients in individual dishes around the noodles. Everyone chooses and mixes their own *antipasto* garnish after they are given a serving of the noodles.

Note: This makes a wonderful cold luncheon dish. Experiment with other ingredients such as chopped hard-cooked eggs or cold chicken pieces, as additions to the noodles.

FUSILLI WITH COLD GARDEN SAUCE

Maria Luisa Scott and Jack Denton Scott

6 servings

This is a unique offering, a cold sauce over a hot pasta. The tricks are two: The pasta must be very hot, and it must be served in hot dishes—we like rimmed soup bowls.

4 MEDIUM-SIZED, DEAD-RIPE TOMATOES, PEELED, SEEDED, COARSELY CHOPPED, PLACED IN A STRAINER AND DRAINED FOR 1 HOUR*
2 CELERY HEARTS, SCRAPED AND MINCED
1 SMALL, SWEET GREEN PEPPER, SEEDED, WHITE RIBS REMOVED AND MINCED
1 SMALL ZUCCHINI, PEELED AND MINCED
3 TABLESPOONS CHOPPED ITALIAN PARSLEY
8 FRESH BASIL LEAVES, CHOPPED
4 TABLESPOONS OLIVE OIL
JUICE OF 2 LEMONS, ABOUT ¼ CUP
1 LARGE CLOVE GARLIC, MINCED
1½ TEASPOONS SALT
1 TEASPOON BLACK PEPPER
1 POUND *FUSILLI* (CORKSCREW PASTA)

1. In a bowl, place all of the ingredients except the pasta and toss, blending well.
2. Cook the *fusilli* in 5 quarts of salted, boiling water until *al dente*. Drain.
3. In a large, hot bowl, place the drained, hot pasta; pour in half of the cold sauce and toss quickly and gently, but well.
4. Serve immediately, while the pasta is still hot, with the remaining cold sauce spooned atop individual servings. We like a cool, young red wine with this and crusty breadsticks. If you still have an appetite, a creamy, warm dessert such as *zabaglione*, or that classic *zuppa inglese* make an excellent follower.

* To keep the sauce from being watery, the tomatoes are drained for an hour, thus eliminating much of the moisture that adds nothing to the flavor or texture of the dish.

Other Pasta Dishes

SPAGHETTI WITH SCALLOPS AND BEURRE NOISETTE

Ruth Spear

4 servings

Pasta dishes may be an Italian invention, but the French do not ignore anything delicious. Here is one superb treatment of spaghetti. The original recipe calls for a tablespoon of finely julienned truffle to be mixed with the ham and tongue. I regard this as consummate lily-gilding, but you may try it if you wish!

¾ TO 1 POUND SPAGHETTI
1 POUND BAY SCALLOPS
FLOUR
7 TABLESPOONS BUTTER
2 TABLESPOONS COOKING OIL
SALT, TO TASTE
PEPPER, TO TASTE
LEMON JUICE
¼ POUND COOKED HAM, JULIENNED*
¼ POUND TONGUE, JULIENNED*
PARSLEY

1. Cook the spaghetti, drain and keep warm.
2. Meanwhile, wash and dry the scallops and roll them in flour.
3. In a skillet, heat 2 tablespoons of the butter and the cooking oil and, when very hot, add the scallops. Sauté them quickly over high heat until pale gold, about 3 to 4 minutes, no longer. (Overcooking results in tough scallops and a loss of flavor.) Turn them into a serving dish, season with salt, pepper and a dash or two of lemon juice, and keep warm.
4. Pour off the fat from the pan in which the scallops were sautéed. Add 3 tablespoons of butter and cook it until it turns light brown, or *noisette* (nut colored).
5. In a separate skillet, melt the remaining 2 tablespoons of butter and briefly heat the julienne strips of ham and tongue.
6. Toss the cooked spaghetti with the ham and tongue, mound it on a heated serving platter and top with the scallops. Pour the *noisette* butter over the spaghetti and garnish with chopped parsley. Serve immediately.

* Buy the ham and tongue in thick slices. The usual paper-thin ones cannot be julienned successfully.

BEEF AND SPINACH RAVIOLI (RAVIOLI À LA NIÇOISE)

Mireille Johnston

6 servings (about 80 ravioli)

Inspired by the dish Marco Polo brought back from China, *raïoles* have been a traditional treat in Provence for centuries. The little squares of dough can be filled with beef, veal, ham, lamb's brains, pumpkin or rice. The Niçois version is truly superb —a savory combination of braised beef, Nice-style, and spinach.

Filling:

2 BOXES (10 OUNCES EACH) FROZEN SPINACH
1 TABLESPOON OLIVE OIL
½ CUP CHOPPED LEAN SALT PORK
1 ONION, GRATED
¾ POUND BEEF, STEWED* AND DICED
1 CLOVE GARLIC, PEELED AND CRUSHED
½ TEASPOON FRESHLY GRATED NUTMEG
2 EGGS, LIGHTLY BEATEN
½ CUP FRESHLY GRATED PARMESAN
1 TEASPOON THYME
SALT, TO TASTE
FRESHLY GROUND BLACK PEPPER, TO TASTE

Pasta:

3 CUPS UNBLEACHED FLOUR
1 TABLESPOON OLIVE OIL
2 EGGS, BEATEN
5 TO 6 TABLESPOONS WATER, APPROXIMATELY
2 TEASPOONS PLUS 2 TABLESPOONS SALT
OLIVE OIL
PARMESAN, GRATED

1. Blanch and drain the spinach; squeeze it dry and chop.
2. In a heavy skillet, heat the olive oil and add the salt pork and onion. Cook for 5 minutes.
3. Place the beef, spinach, and the sautéed onion and salt pork in a blender in three batches and blend to a paste. Or, chop them on a board as finely as possible.
4. Pour this paste into a large bowl and add the garlic, nutmeg, eggs, cheese, thyme, salt and pepper. Check the seasoning and stir well. You should have a smooth and fairly dry mixture.
5. Make the pasta dough. Sift the flour into a large bowl. Make a well in the center and pour in the olive oil, eggs, water and 2 teaspoons of salt. Mix with a fork until all the flour is absorbed, adding another tablespoon of water if necessary.
6. Knead for about 10 minutes, either in the bowl or on a floured table or counter, until the dough becomes smooth and elastic. Form into a ball, place in an oiled bowl, cover with a clean cloth and let rest for 1 hour.
7. Divide the dough into four balls the size of small apples. Roll each ball through the rollers of a pasta machine, following the manufacturer's instructions. Lay the paper-thin sheets of dough on a floured tray or table to dry for about 10 minutes. If you do not have a pasta machine, roll each small ball of dough as thin as possible on a floured board. Let the sheets rest for 10 minutes. (Left any longer they will become difficult to work.)

Continued from preceding page

8. Place a sheet of dough on a floured surface. Put a teaspoon of filling every 2'' along the entire sheet, about 1'' in from the edge; then make another row of filling parallel to the first. Place another sheet of dough on top of the filling and carefully press around each little mound with your fingers, sealing the two layers together. With a pastry wheel, or ravioli cutter, cut around each mound so that you have neat little squares that look like plump cushions. If the pasta strips have become too dry to adhere to one another, dip the pastry wheel, or cutter, into warm water and work them together.
9. When all the squares are cut, sprinkle them with a little flour and allow them to rest for 1 hour before cooking.
10. Bring a large kettle of water to a boil. Add 2 tablespoons of salt and 1 tablespoon of olive oil. Lower the heat and gently slide the ravioli in. Simmer them gently for 5 to 10 minutes. When they rise to the surface, they are ready. Take them out with a slotted spoon and drain them in a colander.
11. In a warm dish, arrange the ravioli, alternating layers of ravioli with a layer of grated cheese and olive oil; or, if there is any sauce left from the beef stew, warm it and use it as a sauce. Serve.

Note: For a variation, if you have roasted a chicken or leg of lamb, deglaze the pan with a little white wine while scraping the bottom of the pan. Use this sauce with the ravioli, which can accompany the chicken or lamb.

* The stewed beef traditionally used for this dish is first marinated in wine with vegetables and herbs, then braised in the marinade with salt pork, garlic, tomatoes, thyme, cloves and orange rind.

MOUSSAKA

Alma Lach

8 servings

2½ TO 3 POUNDS EGGPLANT
FLOUR
½ CUP PEANUT OIL, APPROXIMATELY
¼ CUP OLIVE OIL
1 LARGE ONION, PEELED AND DICED
2 FRESH TOMATOES, PEELED AND DICED (ABOUT 2 CUPS) OR AN EQUIVALENT QUANTITY OF CANNED PLUM TOMATOES
1½ POUNDS LEAN GROUND BEEF
1 TEASPOON SALT
BLACK PEPPER, TO TASTE
½ POUND *FETTUCCINE*
4 TABLESPOONS (½ STICK) BUTTER
5 TABLESPOONS FLOUR
½ CUP HEAVY CREAM
1 CUP WATER
DASH OF NUTMEG
FRESHLY GRATED PARMESAN
2 EGGS
2 TEASPOONS LEMON JUICE

1. Cut the eggplants into ⅜''-thick slices. Peel the slices and drop them into a large bowl filled with enough salted water to cover all the eggplant. Soak the slices for 15 minutes.

---

2. Preheat the oven to 450 F.
3. Drain and blot the eggplant on paper towels, then dredge the slices with flour.
4. Line a baking sheet with heavy foil and coat it with a liberal quantity (about ½ cup) of peanut oil. Arrange the floured slices on the sheet, and then turn them over to coat with oil.
5. Bake the eggplant in the preheated oven for about 20 minutes; turn off the oven, leaving the eggplant inside for 30 minutes.
6. Meanwhile, in a skillet, heat the olive oil. Add the onion and sauté for 1 minute. Add the tomatoes and cook another minute. Then add the ground beef and cook until it is no longer red. Season with salt and pepper.
7. Push the meat mixture to one side of the skillet and prop up the pan under it to allow the oil to drain out of the meat. Spoon out the oil and pour it over the eggplant slices in the oven. Allow the meat mixture to cool.
8. When ready to assemble the *moussaka*, preheat the oven to 350 F.
9. Cook the noodles in a large pot of boiling, salted water. Drain and cool under cold running water.
10. To make the cream sauce, melt the butter in a skillet, stir in the flour, and cook for 1 minute.
11. Add the cream, water and nutmeg and cook, stirring, until very thick. Remove from the heat, cover and set aside.
12. Grease a large (approximately 8'' x 14''), deep, baking dish or two 8'' x 8'' foil cake pans. Arrange alternating layers of eggplant slices, noodles and meat, sprinkling each layer with, and ending with, a layer of Parmesan. Fill the baking dish (or pans) to within 1'' of the top.

    Note: The *moussaka* can be made to this point well in advance and refrigerated or frozen. If frozen, thaw completely before proceeding with the recipe.
13. With a whisk, beat the eggs just enough to blend them thoroughly without making them light. Stir them into the cooled cream sauce, add the lemon juice and mix well. Spoon the sauce over the ingredients in the baking dish.
14. Bake on the bottom shelf of the preheated oven for 45 minutes, or until hot, browned and puffed.

Note: Serve any leftover *moussaka* cold; it is delicious.

SHELLS WITH MUSHROOMS, PEAS AND CREAM

Michael Batterberry

4 to 6 servings

This dish is traditionally made with fresh mushrooms and peas; nevertheless, the following recipe, using staple ingredients, produces a deliciously suave, spur-of-the-moment pasta when you're faced with the challenge of preparing an impromptu meal for company.

½ OUNCE DRIED MUSHROOMS (NOT CANNED)
KOSHER SALT
1 PACKAGE (10 OUNCES) FROZEN "PETITE" PEAS (UNSAUCED)
½ PINT HEAVY CREAM
6 TABLESPOONS (¾ STICK) UNSALTED BUTTER
FRESHLY GROUND WHITE PEPPER
⅛ TEASPOON FRESHLY GRATED NUTMEG
1 TABLESPOON COGNAC OR DRY MARSALA
1 POUND PASTA SHELLS
2 CUPS FRESHLY GRATED PARMESAN

1. Soak the mushrooms in tepid water to cover for 20 minutes.
2. Put on to boil a large pot of cold salted water.
3. In a saucepan, bring ½ cup of water to a boil, salt lightly and drop in the frozen peas. Break them up rapidly with a wooden spoon, then cover the pan when the water returns to a boil. Cook no more than 1 minute, and drain.
4. Reduce the cream to two-thirds of its volume by boiling gently. Add the peas and immediately remove from the heat.
5. Squeeze the liquid from the mushrooms, cut away and discard any woody stems and finely slice the caps.
6. In a skillet, sauté the mushrooms gently for 5 minutes in 2 tablespoons of butter; then add ½ teaspoon salt, 8 grinds of white pepper, the nutmeg and the cognac or Marsala. Stir over high heat until the liquid evaporates, then set aside.
7. Cook the pasta shells *al dente*, according to the package directions, drain well and toss immediately in a heated serving bowl or casserole with the remaining 4 tablespoons of butter, cut into pieces.
8. Quickly add the mushrooms, peas and cream, and 1 cup of the grated Parmesan. Toss well, serve immediately and pass the remaining Parmesan in a bowl.

Note: This dish, which is quite rich on its own, can be made even more so with the addition of a little *prosciutto*, slivered and lightly sautéed for the last 1 minute with the mushrooms (in which case omit the salt in this step).

MACARONI WITH HAM AND CHEESE

Elizabeth Schneider Colchie

4 to 5 servings

3 TABLESPOONS BUTTER
2 SMALL SHALLOTS, FINELY MINCED
3 TABLESPOONS FLOUR
2 CUPS MILK
¾ TEASPOON SALT
¼ TEASPOON PEPPER
¼ TEASPOON NUTMEG
2 CUPS COOKED HAM, CUT INTO ¼" CUBES
1¼ CUPS GRATED JARLSBERG OR GRUYÈRE CHEESE
FEW DROPS OF TABASCO OR OTHER PEPPER SAUCE
½ POUND ELBOW MACARONI
BUTTER
½ CUP FINE, DRY BREAD CRUMBS

1. Preheat the oven to 375 F.
2. In a saucepan, melt the butter; add the shallots and cook a few minutes to soften.
3. Add the flour, stir and cook for 2 minutes.
4. Add the milk, stirring with a whisk, and cook until thickened.
5. Add the salt, pepper and nutmeg and stir. Fold in the ham and cheese and add Tabasco to taste. Set aside.
6. In a large pot of boiling water, cook the macaroni until it is just barely tender. Drain and return to the pot. Add the sauce and mix well.
7. Turn the mixture into a buttered, 6- to 8-cup baking dish, sprinkle with the bread crumbs and dot lightly with butter.
8. Bake, covered with foil, for 30 minutes. Uncover, raise the heat to 425 F. and bake about 10 minutes longer, or until golden and bubbling.

Note: When macaroni and cheese are mixed together and covered with crumbs and butter, the casserole may be sealed with foil and frozen. When ready to use, defrost overnight in the refrigerator, then bake, foil-covered, for 45 minutes at 350 F. Uncover and bake 10 minutes at 425 F.

DANIELLES SPAGHETTI

Maurice Moore-Betty

8 servings

1 POUND SPAGHETTI
½ POUND FRESH MUSHROOMS
5 TO 6 TABLESPOONS BUTTER
SALT
PEPPER
1½ CUPS HEAVY CREAM

1. Preheat the oven to 375 F.
2. Cook the spaghetti in boiling, salted water. Drain and wash under *hot* running water, then drain again. It should be *al dente* to allow for additional cooking during baking time.
3. Wipe the mushrooms with a damp cloth, cut off the stems flush with the cap and chop coarsely.
4. In a heavy skillet, heat 4 tablespoons of butter and cook the mushrooms, stirring, for 2 to 3 minutes.
5. Stir the mushrooms with their pan juices into the spaghetti. Season to taste with salt and pepper.
6. Turn the mixture into a prepared dish and pour on the cream. Do not stir in.
7. Dot with the remaining 1 to 2 tablespoons of butter (according to taste).
8. Bake in the preheated oven for 20 to 25 minutes, or until hot and lightly brown on top.

Note: To make ahead, you may prepare and combine the spaghetti and mushrooms in advance, then pour on the cream and dot with butter just before baking.

COLD SHELLS WITH TUNA

Florence Fabricant

4 servings

Unlike many macaroni-based salads, this one does not become gummy because the starch in the pasta thickens the dressing. The raw vegetables keep everything smooth and moist, making it a good hot-weather dish to prepare in advance.

2 CUPS UNCOOKED MACARONI SHELLS
1 CAN (7 OUNCES) SOLID WHITE TUNA PACKED IN OIL
1 MEDIUM-SIZED TOMATO, PEELED, SEEDED AND CHOPPED
1 MEDIUM-SIZED CUCUMBER, PEELED, SEEDED AND CHOPPED
1 SMALL ZUCCHINI, FINELY CHOPPED
¼ CUP DRAINED CAPERS
2 TABLESPOONS FRESH LEMON JUICE
1 CUP MAYONNAISE
SALT, TO TASTE
FRESHLY GROUND PEPPER, TO TASTE
2 TABLESPOONS MINCED FRESH PARSLEY
1 TABLESPOON MINCED FRESH BASIL

1. Cook the shells in 3 quarts of boiling, salted water until tender. Drain them thoroughly.
2. In a bowl, combine the shells with the tuna, broken into chunks, the oil from the tuna, and the tomato, cucumber, zucchini and capers. Add the lemon juice.
3. Stir the mayonnaise until smooth and fold it into the shells-and-vegetable mixture. Season with salt and pepper.
4. Chill and garnish with the parsley and basil before serving.

SPAGHETTI WITH PÂTÉ DE FOIE GRAS

Michael Batterberry

8 servings

With their inimitable sense of offhanded chic, the Italians occasionally like to startle with a commoner-and-king gustatory marriage. White bean and Beluga caviar salad, for example, or this particular excursion into blasé miscegenation.

1 TIN (14 OUNCES) STRASBOURG LIVER PÂTÉ WITH TRUFFLES* (ABOUT 1 ¾ CUPS)
1½ POUNDS SPAGHETTI, PREFERABLY IMPORTED
5⅓ TABLESPOONS (⅓ CUP) UNSALTED BUTTER
6 TABLESPOONS GOOD COGNAC
1 TO 1½ CUPS TINY CROUTONS OF BEST-QUALITY WHITE BREAD, CRISPED HONEY-BROWN IN BUTTER AND DRAINED
FRESHLY GROUND BLACK PEPPER

1. Chill the pâté to facilitate cutting it into very small bits. Spread these little bits—you can't call them cubes as they refuse to hold their shape—on a buttered plate or on foil, placing them side by side, *not* on top of one another.
2. Boil the spaghetti in a large amount of salted water just until the pasta reaches the firm, *al dente*, stage—*no longer*.
3. While the spaghetti is cooking, melt the butter, add the cognac and simmer for 3 to 4 minutes without allowing the butter to darken whatsoever.
4. Quickly drain the spaghetti and toss in a heated bowl or tureen with the melted butter and cognac.
5. Add the pâté bits and toss, then add the very crisp croutons and toss again.
6. Serve immediately and pass the peppermill for those who can't let well enough alone.

Note: It would be safe to say that few wines are too good for this dish. But to quell indecision, why not settle for champagne?

* If you're willing to go for broke, substitute a similar amount of pedigreed *pâté de foie gras*.

Noodle Dishes

POTATO NOODLES

Florence Fabricant

4 servings

These are of Austrian origin, but are much like the potato *gnocchi* of Italy. My mother learned how to make them from her mother-in-law, and obtaining the recipe was a matter of watching and writing.

1 LARGE BOILING POTATO, PEELED
1 LARGE EGG, LIGHTLY BEATEN
2 TEASPOONS SALT
⅔ TO ¾ CUP FLOUR
1 LARGE ONION, THINLY SLICED AND SEPARATED INTO RINGS
3 TABLESPOONS BUTTER
½ CUP DRY BREAD CRUMBS
1 TEASPOON MINCED FRESH DILL

1. Boil the potato in unsalted water until it is tender. Finely mash it and allow it to cool to lukewarm.
2. Stir in the egg and 1 teaspoon of the salt.
3. Mix in the flour to make a soft dough, being sure to add enough so that the dough is not sticky. The exact amount will depend on the particular potato, the weather, the temperature of the room and so forth.
4. Transfer the dough to a well-floured board and knead lightly for a minute or two.
5. Roll the dough into a rectangle approximately 8" x 12" and ¼" thick.
6. Bring a large pot or kettle of salted water to a boil. At the same time, place the onion and remaining teaspoon of salt in a heavy-bottomed skillet or saucepan, cover tightly and place over low heat to steam until very tender but not brown.
7. Cut the dough into ¼"-wide strips and then cut the strips into 1"-long pieces. You may cook the noodles as is or roll each one lightly to form a slender sausage shape.
8. Drop the noodles into boiling water and boil them about 3 minutes, until they rise to the surface. Drain thoroughly and keep them covered. Do not worry if they stick together.

9. In a large skillet, melt the butter. Add the bread crumbs and stir in the steamed onions and dill. Cook for 2 to 3 minutes.
10. Add the cooked noodles, heat and toss lightly to mix with the crumbs and onions and serve. Sauerbraten, goulash or other hearty stewed dishes served with gravy are perfect with these noodles.

Note: The noodles can be made ahead of time and then frozen. First, lightly dust the uncooked noodles with cornmeal, then place them in a plastic bag and freeze. Frozen noodles may be boiled without thawing. As a variation, 1 cup of finely shredded cabbage or ½ cup of thinly sliced green pepper may be steamed with the onions and then added to the bread crumb mixture.

EGG NOODLES WITH MEAT SAUCE

Florence S. Lin

6 servings

4 TABLESPOONS PEANUT OR CORN OIL
1 POUND GROUND PORK
1 TABLESPOON DRY SHERRY
⅓ CUP BROWN BEAN SAUCE*
2 TABLESPOONS *HOISIN* SAUCE*
¼ TEASPOON MONOSODIUM GLUTAMATE (MSG)
½ CUP CHICKEN BROTH
¼ CUP MINCED SCALLION
1 POUND FRESH OR DRIED EGG NOODLES
3 CUPS BEAN SPROUTS (BLANCHED FOR 30 SECONDS), FINELY SHREDDED LETTUCE, THINLY SLICED CUCUMBER**

1. Heat a wok over moderate heat until very hot. Add 3 tablespoons of oil and stir-fry the pork for about 2 minutes, or until it separates into bits.
2. Splash on the sherry and add the brown bean sauce, *hoisin* sauce and MSG and stir some more.
3. Pour in the broth and bring to a boil. Cook over medium-low heat for about 5 minutes, stirring most of the time.
4. Add the scallion and cook 1 minute longer. Spoon out into a sauce bowl and set aside.
5. Fill a 3- to 4-quart kettle half full of water and bring to a rolling boil. Add the noodles. Stir with chopsticks or a fork, and bring back to a boil; then turn the heat down to medium. Cook for 3 to 5 minutes. Drain.
6. Add the remaining tablespoon of oil to the drained noodles and toss well to keep them from sticking together.
7. Serve the noodles in individual soup plates. Put the lettuce, cucumber or bean sprouts in a serving dish and place it on the table along with the bowl of meat sauce. Each person should help himself to about 2 tablespoons of the meat sauce and some of the garnish, to taste, and mix them well with the noodles.

* These ingredients are available in Oriental markets.

** If you prefer, use 1½ cups each of two of the garnishes.

FRIED NOODLES WITH CHICKEN

Gloria Bley Miller

4 servings

2½ TEASPOONS SALT
½ CUP PLUS 1 TABLESPOON PEANUT OIL, APPROXIMATELY
1 POUND BROAD OR THIN NOODLES
3 TABLESPOONS SOY SAUCE
2 MEDIUM-SIZED, WHOLE CHICKEN BREASTS
2 TABLESPOONS CORNSTARCH
3 TABLESPOONS MEDIUM-DRY SHERRY
1 TEASPOON SUGAR
½ ONION, THINLY SLICED
1 SMALL GREEN PEPPER, SHREDDED
½ CUP CHICKEN STOCK

1. Bring 2 quarts of water to a boil over high heat. Stir in 1 teaspoon of salt and 1 tablespoon of the oil. Add the noodles gradually, to maintain the boiling point, and cook until softened but still firm, about 3 to 5 minutes.
2. Drain the noodles and transfer them to a large bowl. Add 1 tablespoon of the remaining oil and 2 tablespoons of soy sauce to the bowl. Toss to mix, then set aside.
3. Skin and bone the chicken breasts and shred the meat.
4. In a bowl, combine 1 tablespoon of the cornstarch, 2 tablespoons of the sherry and ½ teaspoon each of the remaining salt and the sugar, blending well. Add the chicken shreds and toss to coat.
5. Heat a wok or large skillet. Add 2 more tablespoons of the oil and heat it quickly. Add the chicken and stir-fry over medium heat until the chicken loses its pinkness and turns white.
6. Add the remaining tablespoon of sherry and stir-fry briefly, to blend in.
7. Remove the chicken and set it aside. Rinse the pan.
8. Reheat the wok or skillet. Add 2 more tablespoons of the oil and heat. Add the onion and brown lightly, then add the shredded pepper. Reduce the heat to medium and stir-fry to soften the pepper.
9. Add the stock and ½ teaspoon each of the remaining salt and sugar. Cover and let cook over medium heat, about 3 minutes.
10. Meanwhile, in a cup, combine the last tablespoon of cornstarch, 2 tablespoons of water and the remaining tablespoon of soy sauce, blending well.
11. Return the chicken to the pan with the vegetables and stir-fry a moment to blend in and heat. Add the cornstarch mixture and stir in over medium-high heat, until the liquids thicken. Remove everything from the pan and keep warm. Rinse the pan.
12. Reheat the pan. Add the last 3 tablespoons of the oil and heat until nearly smoking. Add the noodles and heat through over medium-high heat, tossing with spoons or chopsticks.

13. Sprinkle on the last ½ teaspoon of salt and continue tossing the noodles until lightly browned. Transfer to a serving platter. Top with the chicken mixture and serve.

BEEF-NOODLE CASSEROLE

Carol Cutler

8 servings

Every cook needs a good casserole in his repertoire, and this easy one could fill any bill. By adding enough liquid in the baking dish, the noodles do not have to be precooked, thus eliminating one large pot to wash.

3 TABLESPOONS OIL
1 POUND GROUND BEEF
2 MEDIUM-SIZED ONIONS, SLICED
1 CLOVE GARLIC, MASHED
1 CAN (2 POUNDS, 3 OUNCES) TOMATOES
½ CUP TOMATO PASTE
1 CUP RED WINE OR WATER
½ TEASPOON PAPRIKA
1 TABLESPOON SALT
1 BAY LEAF
⅛ TEASPOON THYME
1 TEASPOON MARJORAM
1 TEASPOON WORCESTERSHIRE SAUCE
½ TEASPOON TABASCO SAUCE
½ POUND UNCOOKED BROAD NOODLES
2 CUPS *BÉCHAMEL* SAUCE*
¼ CUP GRATED PARMESAN

1. Preheat the oven to 375 F.
2. In a large, heavy skillet, heat the oil until hot; then add the meat, keeping the heat rather high. Stir the meat with a wooden spoon or fork, breaking it into small pieces.
3. While the meat is cooking, peel and slice the onions. Add the onion and garlic to the meat, cover and simmer for 2 minutes.
4. Add the tomatoes, tomato paste, wine (or water), paprika, salt, bay leaf, thyme, marjoram, Worcestershire and Tabasco sauces. Stir the meat and seasonings well, cover, and simmer for 5 minutes.
5. Select a 2½-quart baking dish, preferably a deep one. Be precise when selecting the baking dish, since the casserole will shrink somewhat as the noodles soften and the finished dish will look rather sunken if prepared in anything larger. Spoon half of the sauce into the baking dish, then add the uncooked noodles. Cover the noodles with the remaining sauce. Spread the *béchamel* sauce in an even layer over the meat sauce.
6. Bake the casserole in the preheated oven for 40 minutes. Sprinkle with the cheese and bake 10 minutes more.
7. Serve directly from the casserole dish.

* The *béchamel* sauce is not added until the final baking, so if you decide to freeze the casserole, do not make the *béchamel* until you are ready to serve it.

JENNIE SHAPIRO'S KUGEL

Kate Slate, with special thanks to Myra Schultz Biblowit

10 to 12 servings

This *kugel* can be served as a side dish in place of potatoes. With just a touch more sugar and fruit, it is also an admirable dessert (*and* late-night snack *and* breakfast *and*....)

SALT
1 POUND BROAD, FLAT EGG NOODLES
3 CUPS RICE KRISPIES
¾ TEASPOON CINNAMON
1¼ CUPS SUGAR, APPROXIMATELY
4 TABLESPOONS (½ STICK) LIGHTLY SALTED BUTTER, MELTED
¾ POUND CREAM CHEESE, CUT INTO CHUNKS AND SOFTENED
1 POUND COTTAGE CHEESE
1 PINT SOUR CREAM
3 MEDIUM-SIZED APPLES, PEELED AND SHREDDED
¾ CUP GOLDEN RAISINS (OPTIONAL)
½ CUP MILK
7 EGGS, LIGHTLY BEATEN
JUICE AND GRATED RIND OF 1 MEDIUM-SIZED LEMON (OPTIONAL)

1. Preheat the oven to 400 F.
2. Grease a 9" x 16" x 1" (or the equivalent volume) baking pan.
3. In a large pot, bring 4 to 6 quarts of water to a rolling boil. Add 1 teaspoon of salt and the noodles. Stir once or twice to separate the noodles. Cook for 10 minutes, until just tender.
4. While the noodles cook, make the topping. Put the rice krispies in a plastic bag and crush them slightly with a rolling pin.
5. In a bowl, toss the crushed cereal with the cinnamon and ¼ cup of the sugar. Add the melted butter and mix in well. Set aside.
6. Drain the cooked noodles into a colander, then rinse them quickly under cold running water. Drain well.
7. Drop the cream cheese chunks into the hot noodle pot. Then put the noodles in on top. Mix thoroughly.
8. Add the cottage cheese and sour cream. Mix well. Add salt, to taste.
9. Add the shredded apples, raisins (if using) and 1 cup of sugar. Taste for sugar and add more if desired.
10. Add the milk and eggs and mix well. Add the lemon juice and rind, if desired, and stir in.
11. Pour the mixture into the prepared pan and sprinkle the top with the crumb mixture.
12. Bake in the preheated oven for 10 minutes. Turn the heat down to 350 F. and bake for 1 hour. Allow to set at least 10 minutes before cutting into squares and serving.

Note: The *kugel* can be reheated at 325 F. for 30 to 40 minutes. It also freezes beautifully after baking. If the *kugel* is cut into squares before freezing, individual portions can be reheated. Thaw completely out of the refrigerator before reheating at 325 F.

NOODLES WITH BATTER-FRIED SHRIMP

Mitsuo Masuzawa

6 servings

- 6 MEDIUM-SIZED JAPANESE DRIED MUSHROOMS*
- 3 TABLESPOONS SUGAR
- 3 TABLESPOONS JAPANESE SOY SAUCE*
- 16 OUNCES PACKAGED *UDON* (WIDE NOODLES)*
- 6 MEDIUM-SIZED SHRIMP (ABOUT 10 OUNCES)
- 1 CUP FLOUR, APPROXIMATELY
- 1 TABLESPOON SALT, APPROXIMATELY
- 1 SMALL EGG YOLK
- ⅔ CUP WATER
- LARGE PINCH OF BAKING SODA
- VEGETABLE OIL
- 2 TABLESPOONS *SAKE*
- 3 OUNCES BONELESS SIRLOIN STEAK, CUT INTO ⅛"-THICK SLICES
- 6 CUPS *ICHIBANDASHI* (SEE BELOW)
- ¼ TEASPOON MONOSODIUM GLUTAMATE (MSG)
- TWELVE ⅛"-THICK SLICES CANNED BAMBOO SHOOTS
- 1 LARGE ONION (6 OUNCES), PEELED AND CUT INTO ¼"-THICK ROUNDS
- TWELVE ¼"-THICK SLICES *KAMABOKO* (STEAMED FISH LOAF)*
- 6 EGGS
- 1 SHEET PACKAGED *NORI* (DRIED SEAWEED)*, CUT INTO 6 SQUARES
- 2 SCALLIONS (INCLUDING AT LEAST 3" OF THE GREEN PART), THINLY SLICED

1. Soak the 6 dried mushrooms in 1 cup of cold water for 15 minutes.
2. Transfer the mushrooms and their soaking liquid to a 1-quart saucepan and bring to a boil over high heat. Add 1 tablespoon of sugar and 1 tablespoon of soy sauce. Lower the heat to moderate and cook for 10 minutes. Set aside.
3. In a 4-quart pot, bring 2 quarts of water to a boil. Add the *udon* and return to a boil. Cook briskly, uncovered, stirring constantly, for about 20 minutes, or until the noodles are very soft.
4. While the noodles are cooking, prepare the shrimp. Shell the shrimp, but leave the tail attached. With a small, sharp knife, devein the shrimp by making a shallow incision down their backs and removing the black or white intestinal vein with the point of the knife.
5. Place about ⅓ cup of the flour and a pinch of salt in a shallow bowl and dredge the shrimp in it; shake off any excess flour.
6. When the noodles are soft, stir in 1 tablespoon of salt, cover the pan tightly and turn off the heat. Let the noodles rest, covered, for 5 minutes. Pour them into a colander and rinse under cold water until they are cool. Drain.
7. In a large mixing bowl, combine the egg yolk, water and baking soda. Sift in ⅔ cup of flour and mix well with a wooden spoon. The batter should be somewhat thin and watery, and should run easily off the spoon. If it is too thick, thin it with a few drops of cold water.

   Note: The batter should not sit for any longer than 10 minutes before being used.
8. Fill a deep fryer, a heavy 10" to 12" skillet or a wok to a depth of 3" with vegetable oil and heat it to 375 F.

Continued from preceding page

9. Dip the shrimp into the batter, then drop it into the hot oil and cook about 3 minutes. Place the cooked shrimp on paper towels to drain and set aside.
10. In a small saucepan, combine the *sake*, sliced steak, 1 tablespoon sugar and 1 tablespoon soy sauce and cook for 2 minutes over high heat. Set aside.
11. In a 2- to 3-quart saucepan, combine the *ichibandashi*, 1 tablespoon sugar, 2½ teaspoons of salt, 1 tablespoon soy sauce, and ¼ teaspoon MSG and bring to a boil over high heat. Lower the heat and keep the broth hot while the rest of the dish is assembled.
12. Divide the noodles equally among six individual heatproof earthenware pots with lids.
13. In each pot, place 1 shrimp, 1 mushroom, 2 slices of bamboo shoot, 2 onion slices and 2 *kamaboko* slices. Divide the steak slices equally among the six pots.
14. Add 1 cup of hot broth to each pot and bring to a boil over medium heat.
15. Add 1 raw egg to each pot, cover and cook over low heat for 2 to 3 minutes.
16. Serve the soup very hot, garnished with a square of *nori* and a sprinkling of scallion slices.

***Ichibandashi* (Basic Soup Stock):**

1 SHEET *KOMBU* (DRIED KELP)*
2½ QUARTS COLD WATER
1 CUP PREFLAKED *KATSUOBUSHI* (DRIED BONITO)*

1. With a heavy knife, cut a 3" square from the sheet of *kombu* and wash it under cold running water.
2. In a 4- to 6-quart pot, bring the cold water to a boil over high heat. Drop in the square of *kombu*. Let the water just come to a boil again, then immediately remove the *kombu* from the pan with tongs or a slotted spoon and discard.
3. Stir the *katsuobushi* into the boiling water and turn off the heat. Let the stock rest undisturbed for about 2 minutes, or until the *katsuobushi* sinks to the bottom of the pan. Skim off any surface scum with a large spoon.
4. Place a double thickness of cheesecloth or a clean napkin in a sieve set into a large bowl. Pour in the stock and let it drain through undisturbed.
5. Remove the *katsuobushi* from the sieve and discard.
6. The stock may now be used as the base for a soup or stew or a cooking base. Although best if freshly prepared for each occasion, *ichibandashi* can be stored, covered with plastic wrap and refrigerated, for as long as two days.

* These ingredients are available in Japanese markets.

WINE NOODLES (WEIN LOKSCHEN)

Raymond Sokolov

4 to 6 servings

2 CUPS FINE NOODLES
1 CUP DRY WHITE WINE
3 TABLESPOONS PLUS 1 TEASPOON SUGAR
3 TABLESPOONS BUTTER
3 EGGS, SEPARATED
1 TABLESPOON GRATED LEMON RIND
JUICE OF ½ LEMON

1. Boil the noodles in salted water until tender. Drain and rinse with hot, then cold water.
2. Preheat the oven to 350 F.
3. Heat the wine with the teaspoon of sugar and mix with the noodles. Cool.
4. Cream the butter, the 3 tablespoons of sugar, egg yolks, lemon rind and juice until smooth. Add to the noodle mixture.
5. Beat the egg whites until stiff and fold into the noodles.
6. Pour the mixture into a well-greased baking dish. Bake for 15 to 20 minutes.

GREEK MACARONI AND MEAT CASSEROLE (PASTICHIO)

Paula J. Buchholz

8 to 10 servings

1½ POUNDS LEAN GROUND BEEF OR LAMB
8 TABLESPOONS (1 STICK) BUTTER
¾ CUP FRESHLY GRATED PARMESAN, ROMANO OR *KEFALOTYRI* CHEESE
3 TABLESPOONS TOMATO PASTE
1½ TEASPOONS GROUND CINNAMON
½ TEASPOON FRESHLY GROUND NUTMEG
SALT, TO TASTE
FRESHLY GROUND PEPPER, TO TASTE
1 POUND *PASTICHIO** NOODLES OR MACARONI, COOKED AND DRAINED

Custard Topping:
12 TABLESPOONS (1½ STICKS) BUTTER
1 CUP FLOUR
3 CUPS WARM MILK
5 EGGS, BEATEN
¾ CUP FRESHLY GRATED PARMESAN, ROMANO OR *KEFALOTYRI* CHEESE

1. Preheat the oven to 350 F.
2. Butter a 9" x 13" baking dish.
3. In a large skillet, brown the meat. Stir in the butter, grated cheese, tomato

Continued from preceding page

paste, cinnamon, nutmeg, salt, pepper and cooked noodles.

4. Turn the mixture into the prepared baking dish.
5. In a saucepan, melt the 12 tablespoons of butter. Stir in the flour until it is well blended, then slowly add the milk and cook, stirring, until the sauce is thickened and smooth.
6. Combine the eggs and the ¾ cup of cheese. Stir the white sauce into the egg mixture and spread on top of the noodles.
7. Place in the preheated oven and bake until a knife inserted in the center comes out clean, about 45 minutes.
8. Let stand a few minutes before cutting into squares and serving. Serve a simple green salad and sliced oranges with this hearty casserole.

* *Pistichio* noodles are a Greek pasta in the form of long, narrow tubes. If you can't find them at an import or specialty food shop, substitute regular macaroni. It works just as well.

BAKED KREPLACH

Jeanne Lesem

3 to 4 servings

Kreplach are Jewish-style noodle-dough dumplings stuffed with a beef filling made from leftover pot roast. They are traditionally served in soup, but my mother sometimes serves them with beef gravy instead, and this recipe, from my Aunt Johnnie, calls for baking after boiling them.

Noodle Dough:
2 CUPS ALL-PURPOSE FLOUR
½ TEASPOON SALT
2 LARGE EGGS
3 TO 4 TABLESPOONS COLD WATER

Filling:
¾ POUND GROUND RAW BEEF OR 1 CUP PACKED, GROUND, COOKED BEEF
1 ONION (ABOUT 2" IN DIAMETER), PEELED AND FINELY GROUND OR CHOPPED
2 TABLESPOONS RENDERED CHICKEN, DUCK OR GOOSE FAT
1 LARGE EGG
1 TEASPOON SALT
FRESHLY GROUND BLACK PEPPER, TO TASTE

OIL OR RENDERED CHICKEN FAT

1. Measure the flour and salt into a large mixing bowl, or into the bowl of a food processor fitted with a steel blade. Break the eggs into the center of the flour in the bowl, or into one side of the processor bowl. Add 3 tablespoons of water. With the fingers of one hand, gradually work the flour into the liquids until you have a stiff but workable dough, or use the processor following the manu-

facturer's directions. If the dough is crumbly, add a little more water. Remove the dough to a board and knead it for about 15 minutes, or until it is smooth and elastic.

2. Cover the dough tightly with plastic wrap and let it rest 30 minutes or more, so the gluten can develop.

3. Meanwhile, make the filling. Mix the ground meat and ground or chopped onions together.

3. In an 8" to 10" skillet, heat the fat. If you are using raw ground beef, brown it with the onions only until the meat loses its pink color and the onions are limp, but not browned. If you use cooked meat, cook and stir it with the onions until the onions are limp, but not browned. Remove the pan from the heat, and let the mixture cool.

5. Mix the egg, salt and pepper into the filling. Divide the filling into 10 to 12 balls and set aside.

6. Divide the dough into two equal pieces. Cover one with plastic wrap, and roll the other to about 1/8" thickness on a lightly floured board.

7. Using a round ravioli stamp, a cookie cutter or a wine glass, mark the rolled-out dough lightly with eight circles. Place a ball of filling in the center of each circle and moisten and edges with water.

   Note: If you use a cookie cutter or wine glass, seal the edges of the dough with lightly beaten egg. The water sealer is sufficient only if you use the ravioli cutter, which is designed to put extra pressure on the edges, and prevent the *kreplach* from breaking open when they are boiled.

8. Roll out the other half of the dough in the same fashion, but do not cut it. Place it over the first layer and the filling and use the cutter to cut and seal the dumplings. At this point, the dumplings may be refrigerated on plates in a single layer for several hours or overnight, if desired.

9. When you are ready to cook the dumplings, bring a large pot of salted water to a boil, drop in the dumplings and simmer them, covered, for about 10 to 15 minutes, until the sealed edges are cooked *al dente.*

10. Remove the dumplings from the water with a skimmer and cool them in a single layer in a large, shallow pan.

11. If you are going to serve the *kreplach* immediately, paint them with cooking oil or rendered chicken fat, place them on a shallow baking pan in a single layer and bake 5 to 15 minutes in a 350 F. oven, or until hot and lightly browned. Otherwise, the dumplings can be refrigerated overnight, or they can be frozen in a single layer and then sealed air-tight in a freezer bag for longer storage. Allow an extra 5 minutes of cooking time if the *kreplach* go straight from freezer to oven.

12. Serve the *kreplach* plain as a snack or accompany them with mustard blended with a little white horseradish. Sour cream tinted pale pink with beet-flavored horseradish also makes an excellent companion. If you serve the dumplings as a main course, green beans, spinach or broccoli go well with them.

Note: You will have scraps of dough left over that you can use up in several ways. I usually chop them as evenly as possible with a knife or pastry cutter. Then I either cook them immediately and serve them with butter and cheese or *pesto*, or I let

Continued from preceding page

them dry, uncovered, for an hour or more, and then cook them. You can also freeze them in a single layer, then bag them and store in the freezer for later cooking.

RICOTTA, SPINACH AND NOODLE PUDDING

Elizabeth Schneider Colchie

3 to 4 main course servings

6 OUNCES (ABOUT 3 CUPS, DRY) EGG NOODLES
4 TABLESPOONS (½ STICK) UNSALTED BUTTER
¾ CUP FINELY CHOPPED ONION
1 PACKAGE (10 OUNCES) FROZEN, CHOPPED SPINACH, PARTIALLY DEFROSTED
½ TEASPOON FINELY MINCED GARLIC
1 POUND WHOLE-MILK RICOTTA CHEESE
⅛ TEASPOON MACE
1 TEASPOON SALT
¼ TEASPOON PEPPER
¼ CUP FINE, DRY BREAD CRUMBS

1. Preheat the oven to 375 F.
2. In a kettle of boiling water, cook the noodles until not quite tender.
3. While the noodles are boiling, cook the onion in a skillet with 1 tablespoon of butter, until softened.
4. Drain the noodles, return them to the kettle and toss with 2 tablespoons of the butter.
5. Add the spinach and garlic and cook, covered, over medium heat for 5 minutes. Uncover and cook a moment to evaporate most of the liquid.
6. To the noodles in the pot, add the onion-spinach mixture, ricotta, mace, salt and pepper and mix well. Scoop the mixture into a rather deep, buttered, 1½-quart baking dish.
7. Melt the remaining tablespoon of butter and stir the bread crumbs into it; sprinkle them evenly over the noodle mixture. Bake in the preheated oven for 45 minutes.

FRIED NOODLES AND ALMONDS

Carol Cutler

4 servings

There is a touch of the thrifty Chinese housewife in this quickly prepared dish. Although you can use leftover noodles (or any kind or pasta), you'll find enough demand for this crisp dish that you'll be boiling noodles especially for it.

4 TO 5 TABLESPOONS BUTTER
½ CUP BLANCHED, SLIVERED ALMONDS
5 CUPS COOKED, DRAINED NOODLES
1 TABLESPOON POPPY SEEDS
FRESHLY GRATED NUTMEG

1. In a heavy skillet, heat 2 tablespoons of the butter and brown the almonds on low heat, turning them often. Remove the almonds with a skimmer when they have turned a dark golden color.
2. Add 1 more tablespoon of butter to the skillet, then the noodles. Turn the heat up to moderate and fry the noodles until crisp, turning quite often. Add more butter if necessary.
3. A minute or so before serving, return the almonds to the pan and add the poppy seeds and a generous sprinkling of nutmeg. Mix all the ingredients thoroughly, then flatten the noodles and do not stir again. Turn up the heat so the noodles on the bottom will brown nicely, frying a minute or two longer.
4. Invert the fried noodles (which will resemble a flat pie) onto a serving platter. Serve with grilled tomatoes and a salad.

Note: This dish can be made heartier by adding julienne strips of boiled ham along with the almonds and poppy seeds.

STIR-FRIED RICE NOODLES WITH SHRIMP AND VEGETABLES

Florence S. Lin

3 to 4 servings

½ POUND RAW SHRIMP, ANY SIZE
½ POUND DRIED RICE NOODLES
2 CUPS SHREDDED CELERY CABBAGE OR FRESH BEAN SPROUTS
2 TABLESPOONS SHREDDED SCALLION
4 TABLESPOONS PEANUT OR CORN OIL
1 TABLESPOON DRY SHERRY
1 TEASPOON SALT
½ TEASPOON SUGAR
1½ TABLESPOONS LIGHT SOY SAUCE
½ CUP CHICKEN BROTH

1. Shell the shrimp, remove the sand veins, split each shrimp lengthwise into halves and wash well. Drain the shrimp, then dry them thoroughly with paper towels.
2. Soak the dried rice noodles in cold water for 5 minutes. Drain well.
3. Set the celery cabbage and scallion on a plate near the stove.
4. Heat a wok over high heat until it is hot. Add the 2 tablespoons of peanut or corn oil, and stir-fry the shrimp in the oil for 1 minute.
5. Splash the sherry on the shrimp, mix well and transfer the shrimp to a dish.

Continued from preceding page

6. Heat the same wok with the remaining 2 tablespoons of oil. Add the scallion and cabbage and stir-fry for 2 minutes; then add the salt, sugar and soaked rice noodles. Fry, stirring, for 2 minutes more. Add the soy sauce and broth. Turn the heat to high and stir-fry until all the liquid is absorbed.
7. Add the cooked shrimp to the noodles and mix well until they are heated through. Serve hot.

NOODLES WITH SPINACH AND MUSHROOMS

Gloria Bley Miller

4 servings

10 DRIED BLACK CHINESE MUSH-ROOMS
½ POUND SPINACH
1 TABLESPOON CORNSTARCH
1 TEASPOON SOY SAUCE
2 QUARTS WATER
1 TABLESPOON SALT
7 TABLESPOONS PEANUT OIL
1 POUND BROAD OR THIN NOODLES
WHITE PEPPER

1. Soften the dried mushrooms in hot water to cover for 30 minutes. Drain, reserving the soaking liquid.
2. Wash and stem the spinach. Cut the leaves in half, if they're large.
3. In a cup, combine the cornstarch, soy sauce and 2 tablespoons of the mushroom soaking liquid and set aside.
4. In a large pan, bring the 2 quarts of water to a boil over high heat. Stir in 2 teaspoons of salt and 1 tablespoon of oil. Add the noodles gradually, to maintain the boiling point, and cook until softened but still firm, about 3 to 5 minutes. Drain.
5. Heat a wok or large skillet. Add the remaining 6 tablespoons of oil and heat quickly. Add the mushrooms and stir-fry to heat through, about 2 minutes.
6. Add the remaining teaspoon of salt and the spinach. Stir-fry to soften, about 2 minutes longer.
7. Add the drained noodles to the pan, tossing—with spoons or chopsticks—to combine with the vegetables and heat thoroughly, about 2 minutes.
8. Stir the cornstarch-soy mixture to recombine, and add to the noodles. Continue to cook, tossing the noodles, until the sauce thickens.
9. Transfer to a serving platter; sprinkle with pepper and serve. Accompany with a light soup for lunch or with a heavier soup for supper.